D0563901

PRINCIPLE MATTERS

11 STRATEGIES FOR HARNESSING YOUR PASSION AND BECOMING AN AUTHENTIC FINANCIAL ADVISOR

ROBERT J. COLLINS

www.principlemattersbook.com

Books are available for special promotions and premiums.
For details, contact :
Special Markets
LINX Corp.
Box 613
Great Falls, VA 22066,
or e-mail specialmarkets@linxcorp.com

Book design by Paul Fitzgerald
Editing by Michelle Johnson
Contributing writing by Sydney Leblanc
Published by LINX

LINX, Corp.
Box 613
Great Falls, VA 22066
www.linxcorp.com

Printed in the United States of America

Dedication

To my legacy, Siobhan,
Your Mom and I love you very much.
We hope you find your passion in life
and go for it.

Disclosure

The experiences described in this book may not be representative of the experience of other advisors and does not constitute a guarantee of any particular advisor's success.

Past performance is no guarantee of future results.

Diversification and asset allocation do not ensure a profit or protect against a loss in a down market.

Dividends are not guaranteed and are subject to change or elimination.

Investing in fixed income securities involves certain risks such as market risk if sold prior to maturity and credit risk especially if investing in high yield bonds, which have lower ratings and are subject to greater volatility. All fixed income investments may be worth less than original cost upon redemption or maturity.

Investing in foreign securities presents certain risks not associated with domestic investments, such as currency fluctuation, political and economic instability, and different accounting standards. This may result in greater share price volatility. These risks are heightened in emerging markets.

Investments that are concentrated in a limited number of securities involve greater risk than diversified investments, because a loss resulting from a particular security's poor performance will have a greater impact on the investments' overall return.

Acknowledgement

I have been very fortunate to get to where I am today in life, and I have many people I would like to acknowledge.

First and foremost I thank my wife, Beth. Despite some bumps in the road, you let me build a career. You have been very patient throughout my long hours away from home, visiting with clients, and phone calls at all hours of the day and night, everywhere and anywhere. You let me go for my passion, and I love you for that and look forward to our future together.

To Mom and Dad (Eileen and Bob), thank you for creating me and molding me in the way you thought was best; I think it worked.

To my close friends and golfing buddies: Joe Tilley, Doug Marks and Tony Guerra, I look forward to many more great conversations about life with you.

To the entire organization of Wheat First Butcher Singer, thank you to this excellent regional brokerage firm for getting my juices going. To my former supervisors... Carlton "Chip" Collins, Bill Weldon and Bob Carr, thank you for all of your support.

To Sydney Leblanc, Michelle Johnson and Chris Marret, thank you for putting my thoughts in writing in order to create this book.

To my team: David Clark, Jordan VanOort, Sally Mullen, Steve Cimino, Stephen Clagett, Esther Ku, Tara Barton, and Kristian Price, thank you for the years of hard work and dedication. Our team's future is very bright!

Table of Contents

Foreword

As someone who has worked in the brokerage business my entire professional career, I didn't think I would ever be rash enough to offer to do something as out of character as writing the foreword for a book. It was during a meeting that both Bob and I were attending, he told me of his plan to write this book, and gave me an overview of the concept, I was so excited about it that I offered on the spot to write the foreword. My excitement stems not just from Bob's description of the book, but also from my knowledge about Bob.

I met Bob a little more than a dozen years ago, when he was practicing at Wheat First Securities, a predecessor to today's Wells Fargo Advisors. Our professional relationship strengthened when Bob decided to establish an independent practice and chose to affiliate it with Wells Fargo Advisors Financial Network, which I head.

A man who is guided by his principles, Bob works hard, is committed to his clients and devoted to his family, and has achieved great success in his profession. Yet, he has managed to stay amazingly humble and down to earth. I believed that Bob's perspective on life would make his insights into professional success all the more valuable, and having read this book, I found I was right.

The "principles" he discusses in this book may not seem all that covert at first glance. The true principles lie in Bob's ability to elaborate, and to provide a common sense perspective that helps to clarify the key role each of these principles plays in making a financial advisor successful. In Chapter 2, for example, when Bob reveals the principles "Know Your Client," Bob underscores the reality that truly successful client relationships are not based on performance, but on trust, and makes the point that people do business with people, not with institutions.

Bob's views on the importance of safeguarding and nurturing one's reputation are shared from the perspective of one who has himself earned a well-deserved reputation for professionalism and high character. That insight is woven throughout the book, but concentrated in a chapter discussing how important it is to "Make a Difference," even when that means going beyond the scope of your "job" to assure that the clients' needs and best interests are pursued. And it's clearly stated in a chapter urging readers to "Follow Compliance," in which Bob notes that, even though it may not always feel like it, "Compliance is your friend."

Each chapter of this book offers guidance that will serve advisors, and ultimately their clients, well when times are good and markets are cooperating. But even more so when they're not. It addresses topics which are fundamental to strong client relationships, and sound human relationships. Readers will put this book down with a better sense of the traits and behavior that underpin success for financial advisors in the 21st century. And, in the process of gaining that knowledge, they'll get a glimpse of the qualities and character that make the author as well liked, as respected, and as successful as he is.

There are many principles in this book, but the fact that I'm proud to call Bob a friend and colleague.

John G. Peluso, Jr
President
Wells Fargo Advisors Financial Network, LLC

Introduction

The truth is that I believe there ARE good financial advisors out there. I believe we exist. I sincerely want to help people manage and grow their wealth and create financial security. I genuinely want to run a company with happy and fulfilled employees. And, I want you to know about it. Why? Because the good guys (and gals) are still out there. It isn't always the easiest way to be in this industry, and sometimes, tough calls need to be made. But, ultimately, I go home each night confident that I made the right choices for my clients and the right choices for me and my team. In the end, it isn't always about making that buck. It's about doing what's right.

My goal for writing this book is that after you read it, you will realize that a financial advisor is not just someone entrusted to manage money. People trust you with their money, yes, but they also trust you with their stories, their secrets, their mistakes, and their fears. Being a true financial advisor means so much more than just seeking to make a profit for your client or a profit for yourself. An authentic advisor is someone who can see beyond the potential quick return, and embrace the true meaning of a total return. My passion stems from the excitement of managing money, yet it also comes from the knowledge that I am playing a role in people's lives and helping secure their financial futures.

> *"Never give up, for that is just the place and time that the tide will turn."*
>
> — Harriet Beecher Stowe,
> abolitionist and author (1811-1896)

When I really examined my business, this industry, and my life, I realized that my success and happiness has stemmed from several very simple, yet fundamental principles. Of course, there are those in our industry who play the stock market and rely on the "hot tip" of the day. But if you really want to build a solid and successful career, it takes more than just a hot tip. It takes perseverance. It takes compassion. It takes passion. It takes belief in yourself and knowing what is right. It takes trust, and it also takes the wisdom and insight of knowing when to let go.

I didn't set out to write a book. But, as I came to these conclusions, I realized that others might benefit from the often very simple, yet necessary, lessons I've learned throughout the years. So, I decided to go for it. This is the result. This is my story. In reading this book, I hope you will see that it is possible to make a difference in someone's life by doing something you love to do; and, that there is always hope – even when odds are stacked against you. I want my story to inspire you to keep fighting for what you know is right, as I believe you will be rewarded in the end. I want my story to motivate you – no matter what *your* story is – to go for it and don't give up!

Chapter 1
Find Your *Passion*

PRINCIPLE #1: Find your passion. Sounds cliché, perhaps. But, arguably, it is the most important "principle" to succeeding in your life. If you aren't passionate about what you do, you aren't going to be successful in doing it. With that said, finding your passion doesn't always happen at the most fortuitous or most convenient moment. Sometimes you know what you want to do from childhood on; sometimes you figure it out later in life. I realized what my passion was as a senior in college. I suppose the small miracle in that was primarily the fact that I barely had made it to my senior year at all.

Looking back, it's hard to believe that I was the consummate C+ student throughout high school and part of college. I didn't pay much attention during my classes while in high school, and I got into the University of Scranton by the skin of my teeth. And, at the end of my first semester I had earned a 2.1 GPA…0.2 percent away from academic probation. But, as I continued my education at the Jesuit college in Pennsylvania, something started to click for me. I realized that by attending the University of Scranton I was learning how to truly compete in the world, and I was encouraged by the Jesuits to move ahead with my dreams. I understood, as a result of my education there, that I was a part of something much larger than myself. It made me want to "give back" to my community, which, in turn, fostered the feeling of belonging and accomplishment. This desire to give back, and the confidence to go for my dreams, was cultivated during my years at the University of Scranton, and it is the foundation upon which I continue to build my life to this day.

Confidence and giving back are easier when you are an established business owner, but having the guts to go for a dream when you are just a college kid is a lot different. I was really tested during my last year in school, when, as a senior year accounting major, I attended a seminar where the key speaker was a stockbroker named Greg Thompson, a University of Scranton alumni and one of the original "stock jockeys". Stock jockeys constantly trade—they love it and live for it—for their clients (if suitable) and for their own account. Greg worked for a DC firm founded in the

70s—Moseley, Hallgarten, Estabrook, and Weeden—and he gave a passionate lecture to our business class describing his life and career in the securities industry "fast lane". I was awestruck by his ability and thought to myself, "I'm changing my game plan immediately."

See, a degree in accounting was a safe bet. I wasn't overwhelmingly passionate about accounting, but I knew it was a solid career choice. But being a stockbroker? A stock jockey? Life in the fast lane? Now that sounded like a lot of fun. I could get revved up by that! A stockbroker I would be. But deciding on my career wasn't the hardest part. No, the hardest part was telling my parents (I'm sure most of you can relate). So, during my last semester of college, I made plans to go home to see my folks in Northern Virginia. Soon after I arrived, I made my big announcement. "Mom, Dad: I'm not going to be an accountant. I'm going to be a stockbroker." My dad beamed and encouraged me, as he always had, to "go for it." My mom, on the other hand, wasn't quite as easily convinced (fast-forward 29 years...my mother is my biggest supporter! She has stuck by me through every triumph and every crisis, and her loyalty is a huge inspiration to me).

With breaking the news to my parents behind me, I was free to embark upon my new career.

As graduation loomed, I scoured the want ads for stockbrokers, and one firm that caught my interest was

First Jersey Securities. I cut out the ad and held on tightly to it through the summer after graduating from college, while I worked as a foreman for my uncle's construction firm to earn a little income while I stayed with my folks. I kept thinking about being a stockbroker and how much I wanted to join a securities firm. I didn't even know the difference between First Jersey, Merrill Lynch, Dean Witter, or EF Hutton, but I still had that tattered want ad for First Jersey. I figured I would start there. At the time, interest rates were over 15%, the Dow Jones was around 850, and unemployment was over 10%. The job market for college grads at the time was very tough. So, when I finally made that call to First Jersey, I was lucky enough to get an interview for an entry-level stockbroker position at their Bailey Crossroads office. To my delight, I GOT THE JOB! It wasn't a salaried position, but it was a job! Needless to say, I was thrilled. I studied the remainder of the summer for my Series 7 license, passed the test, and started my career as a stockbroker in September 1982.

I reported for duty bright and early that first day but was dumbfounded at the sight as I walked through the front office door. The entire office was filled with rows and rows of desks lined up, nice and straight. There must have been about 40 desks in all; all occupied by young, energetic men. The office manager showed me to my desk and dropped a heavy Yellow Pages phone book on top of my desk with a loud thump. "Here's your prospect list and here's your script. Call all the gasoline station owners, and we'll tell you what to say. Just memorize the script."

So here I am—a naïve, wide-eyed kid right out of college—holding a phone book. I believe I am a fairly smart guy, but I had absolutely no idea what was going on. I felt I had been blind-sided. I had to find my own prospects. Call gas station owners? Read a script? I wanted to buy and sell stocks, just like Greg Thompson told us he did during his lecture at the University of Scranton Career Services Night. I thought I would be learning how to help clients make money, but this was no better than being a door-to-door vacuum cleaner salesman. I was disillusioned, disappointed, and full of anxiety by the end of the day. When I left that evening, I thought to myself, "If this is the stock business, I'm not doing THIS for a career. How does this help *anyone*?"

Later that evening, while having dinner with my parents, I turned to them—defeated and with tears in my eyes—and announced, "I'm quitting." Both mom and dad stared at me for a moment in disbelief. They certainly weren't expecting to hear *that* from me. They were, instead, expecting to hear how happy I was and how great my first day on the job went. After I explained my day of cold-calling gas station owners, my dad said, "Give it a chance, give it a little more time and hang in there. After all, it's just your first day." And what did my mom say? You guessed it. She said to my father, "I TOLD you so. He should have gotten a real job."

I didn't need to hear that, for sure, but my parents didn't raise a quitter.

Begrudgingly, I went back to the office on Tuesday, sat at my desk, and proceeded to cold-call. The branch manager spent his day walking back and forth in front of the rows of desks yelling and screaming, "Go get 'em guys!" Some motivation, huh? There was no incentive to get to know your customers, and there certainly wasn't any stock analysis available. The stock we were pushing was selling for 43 cents per share, and I was receiving a commission of 15 cents per share. I thought that was a big spread. So, after a few more hours of cold-calling, and a few more hours of thinking over and over in my head how nuts this was, I decided to make a few calls on my own volition. Instead of gas station owners, I started making calls to large retail brokerage firms like Merrill Lynch, EF Hutton, and Smith Barney to sell myself! I needed to work for a real firm and be an actual stockbroker. I wanted to be the guy who was actually helping his clients secure their futures. The cold-calling thing was not for me.

Back in those days, there were a seemingly unlimited number of retail brokerage houses, or wirehouses as we call them. Today, many of them have merged or gone under. I continued calling firms for interviews, and even though I had my Series 7 license, nobody wanted to interview me because I had no prior sales experience. Plus, being just a regular kid from the suburbs, I had no family money or connections, two other things firms back then liked in their new hires. But I was determined. And suddenly it dawned on me—I'll call the guy that unknowingly started me down this career path, Greg Thompson. So, I called up Greg's firm, Moseley Hallgarten, in DC! Happily, I got an interview and met with Greg and the branch manager in downtown DC I explained the entire situation and my overwhelming desire to be a successful stockbroker. I told the manager about Greg's lecture back at Scranton and how impressed I was, and that it was after listening to that lecture that I decided this was going to be my lifelong profession. By the end, I actually pleaded with the manager, "I want out of First Jersey, this is not the kind of firm I want to be affiliated with. I want to be with a REAL firm!" I had on my best suit, and gave him my best and most heartfelt argument for wanting to work for Moseley. He listened politely. Then he said one word: **"NO."**

What? Was I hearing right? Here I have my Series 7, I graduated from the same university as did their big producer, Greg Thompson, and the branch manager is turning me down? I was devastated. I was just a young guy out of school wanting to make a mark on the world, and I felt like I was hitting nothing but brick walls. The thought of quitting on my dream career before it even started crossed my mind in those moments. Then the branch manager scribbled down a name and number on a piece of note paper, handed it to me, and said, "Call this firm, and maybe they can do something for you. Good luck."

The brokerage firm was Laidlaw, Adams, and Peck in Rockville, Maryland. I wasn't totally familiar with them, so I did some research to find out more. Encouraged by what I researched, I called them right away and landed an interview at the branch manager's home in Great Falls, Virginia on a Saturday afternoon, just five days after my first day at First Jersey! I was cautiously optimistic. When I arrived for my appointment, he greeted me at the door wearing shorts and a t-shirt—and here I am in my best suit! I followed him to his sunroom where he interviewed me, and we talked for a while. That was my lucky day. Maybe it was my suit, or maybe it was my willingness to drive to his house on a Saturday for an interview. Whatever it was, he hired me on the spot, right there in his sunroom! And that is when my career actually began.

That Monday, after turning in my resignation to First Jersey, I began working for Laidlaw. It was a "real" firm with about 20 brokers in the branch, most of them experienced, and a couple of young rookies with a few years in the business. I watched what they were doing the first day or two, and then the broker sitting at the desk next to me showed me an ad promoting tax-advantaged bonds that he had placed in *The Washington Post*. It was a small, inexpensive ad, but he was receiving a lot of calls on it. I definitely took note of this advertising opportunity.

Meanwhile, as the weeks went by at Laidlaw, I was spending my time doing direct mail promotions: basically sitting at my desk all day folding, stuffing, licking, and mailing these promotional/sales pieces. After a few weeks, I decided to take a page out of my fellow broker's marketing playbook and run a newspaper ad together with a younger broker in my office. We split the cost of the ad, which was approximately $500. Well, the ad ran in the paper, and the calls started coming in. We were both receiving calls from investors who were willing to invest with us on the first call. I was astounded that people would just give a total stranger money to invest without meeting them first. I couldn't help but think that I really needed to go out and meet these prospects and clients. I wanted them to know me, feel comfortable with me, and trust me. From that trust, we could build a solid, long-term relationship. Even a few weeks into my career, something in me just believed that was the way to build a successful career in this business. The passion for this career, and for those investors who would become lifelong clients, had already taken root in me.

With the success of the ads that I ran in the newspaper, and the contacts and relationships I began building, I'm happy to say I never had to cold-call again. The ad campaigns were great, and I had a lot of success running the ads on Sunday in the business section of the paper. Sometimes I would partner with another advisor, and we would open the office on Sunday from 9:00 a.m. to 1:00 p.m. Sometimes we would receive as many as 50 phone calls, and most of the callers usually had money to invest.

During my first full year as a stockbroker, I made $110,000 in gross commissions, and 80% of it came from municipal bond sales. This was about $44,000, or a 45% payout back then. I figured that I would take 30% of my earnings and invest in more print ads. So, for the first few years of my career, I ran ads every Sunday and Tuesday in *The Washington Post, The Richmond Times,* and *The Baltimore Sun.* I always wondered why more firms and advisors did not do this. Were they just cheap? Did they not want to work on a Sunday? Whatever their reasons, it worked out great for me because then I didn't have to fight off too much competition!

As my first year as a broker came to an end, I was pleased with what I had accomplished. In those days, bonds yielded up to 15% and almost sold themselves. The bond business was definitely good to me that first year, and it still is today.

In fact, after just one successful year, the competition was already hearing about me—the impressive rookie at the Laidlaw Rockville, Maryland branch. And guess who comes knocking at my door? Yep, it was "Mr. No" from Moseley. Now that I knew what I was doing, he wanted me at his branch. He tried everything; I heard it all. They even offered $10,000 up front, and that was huge money back then. My parents urged me to make the move to Moseley. But I said to them, "Absolutely not. They had a chance to hire me and they didn't. Laidlaw took a chance on me and I owe it to them to stay. Plus, I'll make much more than $10,000 this year at Laidlaw." Sure enough, my second year in the business I earned about $140,000 in gross revenues. Back in 1984, and especially for someone a few years out of college, this was good money.

A few years later, opportunity came knocking again. Our Laidlaw branch manager and a few other advisors in the office decided to open up a Dominick & Dominick franchise (an old-line brokerage firm founded in 1870). All my buddies were leaving, so I decided to go, too (we eventually merged with a local firm called Riviere Securities which, in turn, created Atlantic Regional Securities). I soon became one of their biggest producers by continuing to advertise and market my business. By the beginning of the 1990's, I had built it up and was grossing $300,000 and holding $30 million in assets under management (AUM).

However, unbeknownst to me at the time, there were several advisors in my office who were involved in some business I considered to be unethical. Although their practices weren't necessarily illegal, I didn't feel comfortable with the path these guys were going down, and I knew I couldn't stay there. So, by 1992, I decided I had to leave Dominick & Dominick. There were a few really solid regional firms who wanted me, namely Legg Mason Wood Walker, and Wheat First Butcher Singer. I chose Wheat for two reasons: they offered me $30,000 which was a good rate at the time, and because of a fellow named Carlton "Chip" Collins (no relation). I liked his humble style. Wheat First Butcher Singer had a southern conservative regional feel where I knew I could grow. My gut said to go for it. A lot of my decisions are made with my gut, and in this case, my gut was right.

I began working at Wheat First Butcher Singer in March of 1992. I was there about a month when I learned that the firm was sending their top brokers to Switzerland. Chip Collins invited me to go and I jumped at the chance. So, barely two months into working for my new firm, my wife and I were in Switzerland, hanging out with all of the top Wheat First Butcher Singer guys. It was during this trip that I came to a conclusion: I realized that these successful brokers were just like me! It was then that I truly knew I could do just as well as they were doing. It was a wonderful trip. They wined and dined us, and we got a real taste for the good life.

The trip was a real turning point for me. It made me believe that I could achieve the high goals I set for myself. I saw the hunger and passion those top producers had, and I knew I had it in me, too. Later that year, the firm developed the Top Gun program for rising brokers. Chip, looking out for me again, got me in the door to this select group, which consisted of about 15 brokers who were grossing $250,000+ annually. The firm would host Top Gun meetings at the Wheat headquarters. During those meetings, we all stayed at the historic Jefferson Hotel in Richmond, which was built in 1892 and has a 5-Star and 5-Diamond rating. Legend even has it that the grand staircase in the lobby was featured in the movie, *Gone with the Wind.* The Top Gun program culminated in a four-day event, which included mingling with several million-dollar producers from the firm.

I'll never forget meeting and mingling with those successful brokers, and what I learned from them. They each had their own styles and different books of business. Two of them, Larry Boggs and Don DeWees, Sr., each had developed successful practices that were unique to them. Larry Boggs (who eventually became my early mentor) lived in Cumberland, Maryland, which is in the Maryland countryside, and not exactly considered a gold mine of potential investors. But he was a million-dollar producer nonetheless, and he enjoyed working with smaller accounts—lots of them! Don DeWees, a big bond guy, had years of experience and was just transitioning to the money management business. So, as I picked the brains of all these million-dollar producers for four days in this lavish hotel setting, I came to one conclusion: I can do that!

The brokers in our Top Gun group were all competitive, and we competed to be the first to hit the $1 million mark in gross commission. I'm proud that I was the second in the group to reach the goal. The Top Gun guys really bonded, and we became good friends. After all this time I am still in touch with a few of them, and they are all successful financial advisors today. I believe our individual success in this business was spurred on with that early Top Gun program. It really motivated me and gave me tools that I still use to this day. I think every advisor should have the chance to learn these tools and have the opportunity to be motivated and mentored from the ground up. That's one of the reasons I wanted to write this book—to give back in some way what I was given so many years ago. I want to use my story to motivate you, whether you are several years into your career or a rookie just starting out. The truth is I believe you CAN do it, whatever your "it" is. Because that drive; that passion? It's inside each of us. All you need to do is go for it!

Chapter 2
Know *Your Clients*

PRINCIPLE #2: Know your clients. This is honestly the single most important principle I follow in my business. Many people don't realize that real success is less about performance and more about relationships. Forming relationships with your clients is of utmost importance, regardless of what business you are in.

As financial advisors, it is our job to know about our clients' assets; it is our job to know the gains and losses on their accounts and whether they are looking for a quick return, steady income, or a total return. But what I am talking about is actually getting to know *them*. You know, as people. When was the last time you visited a client at their home, shared a meal, asked about their kids, their dogs, their golf game? Do you know what makes your clients tick? Do you know what type of service they expect or want? Because knowing these things—that's how you build relationships that last the duration.

My time in the Top Gun program at Wheat First Butcher Singer was an important part of my career. It helped catapult me into the "big leagues", so to speak. But, the most important thing I learned—and continue to learn—was to put my clients first. Even as a young broker, I understood the importance of having passion as well as a moral commitment to my clients. And, looking back on my career, of course I'm proud of my accomplishments in this industry, but I am most proud of providing exceptional service to those clients who place their trust in myself and my team every day. Trust is the cement that binds your clients to you for the long term. We hear this a lot in our business but, unfortunately, many times it *is* simply lip service. For this reason, it may be difficult at times to convince prospective clients that you will put their best interests first. Yet, with persistence, humility, and honesty, you can *show* them that you are serious. All this begins with getting to know them.

In the early days when I was gaining clients from my bond advertising, I would drive out to see prospects and clients and just knock on their door. These days the average advisor doesn't visit a client at home. It's a shame, because they are missing out on a wonderful experience. I still love getting on the road, driving to their residence, meeting the family members, sitting at that kitchen table. It is a chance to observe and understand how the clients really live. By meeting in person, whether it's at their home, their office, at a restaurant, or on the golf course, you get a better feel for what they are all about. Plus, you make the clients feel special and are giving them excellent service. And, when I do visit my clients or prospects, I just sit back and let them talk (something else I picked up years ago as well). I can quickly determine what's on their mind and help take care of any problems or challenges, or simply help put them at ease. By giving clients attention and understanding, their trust in you grows. The more people trust you, the more they will recommend you to a business associate, friend, or family member. Hence, knowing your client is not just a great business practice, it is another great way to develop your reputation.

Many times, as I get to know my clients or prospects, I find myself developing friendships with them. It is a natural progression given the nature of our business in the financial services industry. In my opinion, people often place more trust in their financial advisor than they do their doctor or lawyer. There's no better way to truly know your client than to be able to count them as a friend.

Passion for my work is what drives me to succeed; it brings me great joy knowing I am helping my clients achieve financial freedom and success. But *knowing* my clients enables me to see what needs to be done for them, even when they may not see it themselves.

I have a client who, over the years, has become a good friend. Let's call him Joe. At 58 years old, Joe was faced with a challenge. He was a successful insurance agent with a strong practice. But, as he neared his 60th birthday, he was getting tired and, after a lifetime of building his insurance agency, he decided he was ready to head in a different direction. His challenge? He was worried about running out of money. Joe actually had plenty of assets, but he just didn't realize it. He didn't feel secure enough financially to walk away from his business (his security blanket) and enjoy retirement. Unfortunately, as Joe contemplated his move toward retirement, he was diagnosed with prostate cancer. Now, even more was at stake; we weren't just talking about his business, we were talking about *his life*.

More than ever, I felt that I needed to help Joe understand his retirement options. I wanted to illustrate to him that enjoying retirement had less to do with returns in the stock market—it all had to do with cash flow. I explained that he had assets that could generate potential cash flow and that, in my opinion, he shouldn't touch the principal. In order for him to have a "roadmap" of sorts, I created an Envision® plan for him (available through Wells Fargo Advisors Financial Network, and something I will explain in more detail later on), representing his current level of progress toward his financial goals at any given time. This plan continuously looks at a client's net worth, time horizons, and risk tolerance, and can be readily adjusted as circumstances change. Joe and I talked at length about his options, and I tried my best to assure him that he would be taken care of in retirement. Finally, with the help of the Envision® plan's documented cash flow potential generated by his investments, our many conversations, and the urgency of his medical condition, Joe was finally convinced to make the decision to sell his agency.

Ultimately, I believe it was our phone conversations and our conversations on the golf course, which convinced him. It was necessary to reassure him and to discuss the realities of the current economic environment. He needed someone right there, showing him facts and details. Since he was a very intelligent businessman, I had to seek to understand him financially and intellectually. I had to relate to his circumstances, his insecurities, his fears. Joe listened to my advice. Today, he is healthy and in semi-retirement enjoying himself. He continues to thank me for giving him the push he needed to take that leap. A sincere thank-you is a wonderful reward. But it took knowing this client, insecurities and all, to manage Joe's money and assist him in achieving his financial dreams.

Many times, we have to wait for the client to come to us with a specific need before we can help them. Recently, a long-time client called and asked if I could refer him to a good insurance agent. I said, "Henry, why do you need a insurance agent?" He explained that he needed someone to sell him long-term care insurance because he was worried about the future. I told him, "Henry, I can sell you long-term care insurance. But why do you think you need it?" I went on to explain the benefits and risks of long-term care insurance and the option to self-insure. Henry and his wife were appreciative that I was there to advise them on this important life decision. They were able to make changes in their portfolio, and I was able to help them feel confident in their decision to self-insure.

Knowing your clients, and being able to work with them to address their individual financial needs, will benefit everyone. They receive expert advice and financial services, and your business has the potential to grow. Plus, you can feel good knowing you are helping people put their financial concerns to rest.

Yet, despite your best efforts, be prepared for some hesitation from clients from time to time in this business. Especially in light of what we have experienced in our industry over the past few years. Now more than ever, your actions as a financial advisor truly do speak louder than words. With Ponzi schemes, a volatile stock market, and the worst economy in years dominating the headlines, investors are frightened, many with good reason. They may believe that the advisors they have trusted in the past may no longer be trustworthy. The scandals involving some in the financial services industry have served as fodder for many to blame everyone in our industry. As a result, too often the hard-working, ethical advisors get a bad rap. Well, guess what? It is up to us to "prove" that we are trustworthy. Our clients and prospective clients deserve trustworthy advisors, and we must do what it takes to earn their trust. We can do that through our actions, our experience, our background, our references, our track record, and our endorsements. You must (and I mean MUST) exceed your client's expectations at every level, every step of the way.

What started after the housing bubble burst was systemic and spread throughout our economy and financial markets like wildfire. But, through it all, my team and I (and thousands of other financial advisors) stayed close to our clients. What astonished me was when the market was in the middle of the meltdown in 2008–2009, clients were actually calling us to ask if WE were doing okay. Can you believe that? I felt terrible when some of my clients took losses, even though I believe it was often beyond my control. And during the Lehman Bros. crisis…well, I was literally sick to my stomach. I couldn't sleep at night, and I felt as though I personally had let my clients down. But, those feelings just further illustrated to me how much I *do* care about my clients. It is that emotion that is at the heart of the client-advisor relationship and why it is so important for you to know your clients and give them service that they deserve.

Here is an example of the kind of service that clients appreciate. A few months ago, one of my clients, Doug, received a letter in the mail that concerned a bond he had purchased. It happened to include the word "bankruptcy" in the text (albeit unrelated to Doug's bond). Reading the word bankruptcy, Doug panicked and called one of the associates on my portfolio team on his cell phone to voice his concerns. My associate was home, but he was on his way out for the evening, and so he immediately sent me a text message that said, "We have an issue; please call me right away." Within 10 minutes, I had conferred with my associate and called Doug to explain everything to him. I felt great that I was able to comfort him. We had another brief conversation first thing in the morning, and afterward I emailed him some facts and other information. My point is: Not only do you have to give that kind of exceptional service to increase your own reputational value, but you also must understand that this is not a 9–5 job. In order to create a successful practice, you need to be prepared to work a 24-hour job. Basically, you are "on call" (this frustrates my wife from time to time, but after 25 years of marriage, she's finally getting used to it!).

Another thing to keep in mind is that the client-advisor relationship goes both ways. You have to be open with them to develop a good dynamic. For example, most of my clients know I have a daughter named Siobhan and that she is a swimmer. As she was leaving for college several years ago, a lot of clients asked me, "Where's your daughter going to college? Is she still swimming?" It was always nice to hear these questions from clients because I knew they were genuinely interested in what was happening in my life. Years ago, there were many days when I drove my daughter to her school at 5:00 a.m. so she could swim from 5:30 a.m. until her school day started at 8:00 a.m. I would read *Barron's Magazine* or *The Wall Street Journal* while she was swimming. That was our routine for about five years until she got her driver's license. I share these wonderful times with my clients, and they feel as though they are following my growth as an individual and as a parent. They like knowing I'm married, have a family and live a "normal" life, much as they do. They can tell I love my family, and that I am sincerely interested in them and their families, too.

The bottom line is that I treat my clients the way I want to be treated. Anyone reading this needs to understand that clients just want to be treated with respect and with honesty. Clients know when you are not sincere, and when you are not showing them your heartfelt gratitude for their business. One thing I came to appreciate a long time ago is this: *When a client is paying me a fee or a commission, then they should expect—and receive—the highest level of service and commitment from me and my team.*

Almost three decades ago, as I mentioned in Chapter One, when I first entered the business, I was selling bond investments and essentially just trying to make it. But as time went on, I realized it wasn't only about making money, it was about building a career, and the only way to build a superior career is if the clients know you are on their side. When I said that this business is not just about making money, I meant it. The money made by a successful advisor can be very good, but I look at my income now more like my "report card". It tells me if I'm doing a good job for my clients. Twenty-nine years ago it wasn't about a report card—it was about trying to earn a living. I was a salesman: a broker selling investments. But now, my business model has changed to one of a full service financial advisor, and I practice exceptional standards of care with my clients. I want to leave a legacy of trust and respect when I retire from this industry as I'm sure you do, too. Therefore, I urge you to take this "principle" to heart. If you build *friendships* instead of just business relationships, you are taking the fastest, and I believe most rewarding, road to success.

Chapter 3
Make a *Difference*

So far, I have passed along two "principles" of success: find your passion and know your clients. **Principle #3** takes both passion and knowledge of your client to the next level and underscores the fact that being successful isn't always about making money. It's always about making a difference.

I'll wager that as kids, most of us were taught to "do the right thing", and "treat others as you want to be treated". And when you are a child that really isn't too hard; be nice on the playground and share your cookies at snack time. But, as we get older, doing the right thing isn't always as easy or as apparent as it was in elementary school.

As a financial advisor, your goal is to grow your clients' assets and work with them to achieve their financial goals. Of course, this alone makes a difference to our clients. They appreciate the work we do to secure their futures, and you are satisfied knowing you have done your job well. But sometimes, helping a client goes beyond the typical scope of a financial advisor. Sometimes you may need to step up and take on situations because you know it is the right thing to do, regardless of whether it is outside the scope of your "job". It's during these times when you can truly make a difference in someone's life.

Frieda has been my client for almost two decades. For all that time, Frieda has never been what you would call an easy client. Actually, Frieda isn't exactly what I'd call an easy person at all. Yet, Frieda is one client that taught me one of the most important lessons of all. In the end, life is about doing the right thing for another human being, because you know you can make a positive difference in that person's life. So, who *is* Frieda? Never married and childless, Frieda spent her adult life working as a bookkeeper and stashing away every extra cent. To say she was frugal is an understatement. She had few friends and was estranged from her only family, a brother. Difficult and opinionated, she led a very reclusive and lonely life. Frieda came to me in 1993 with a modest life savings, and I have worked with her ever since.

Never a spender, Frieda lived on the bare minimum—buying all of her clothing at thrift stores, refusing to indulge on vacations or any luxuries. She never wanted to spend any of the dividend checks she received; instead, she would simply deposit the checks and send one right back to me for reinvestment. She loved receiving those checks. Frieda's primary purpose became building her portfolio, and, as the years progressed, she sought to substantially grow her once-modest life savings. During this time, Frieda latched onto a goal: to be worth a million dollars. The idea that she, a daughter of a poor taxi driver and a housekeeper, could one day boast a seven-figure portfolio was thrilling to her.

After many years as my client, Frieda started exhibiting some strange behavior. By now in her mid-70s, she would call our office and ask to speak to her mother (who had passed away more than two decades prior) or to see her long-dead father. She would talk to me for hours and cry about never being married, never being kissed and how myself and my team were the only people she trusted in the world. In fact, she became very attached to me—even naming a pet bird Bob, after yours truly.

Yet for every endearing thing Frieda did, she did ten more things that frustrated myself and my team. As financial advisors, you can usually overlook occasional rudeness directed towards you, but clients that are mean to your team members are not acceptable. I had to have many talks with her about her treatment of my team. At one point, her behavior was so poor, I gave my team the option to "fire" her as our client. In spite of her rude and frustrating behavior, my team and I decided to stick it out with Frieda. We knew that our group was the closest thing she had to a family, and none of us could bear to turn our backs on her, especially when she needed us most.

In 2003, I met with Frieda to discuss her portfolio and her future. As we discussed the future, she burst into tears, worried that she had no one to take care of her in her last years. She was so afraid and alone. I reassured her that, when the time came, I would be there to help her with her finances. But Frieda wanted something more. She wanted people to know who she was, even long after she was gone. And so I asked her, "How do you want to go about doing that?" Frieda said, "I want to have a hospital wing named in my honor." I explained to her, "Frieda, your current portfolio won't do it; you're going to need a lot more than a million bucks to build a hospital wing." So Frieda said, "Well, find another way."

After thinking it over, I suggested that Frieda start a scholarship fund. She loved the idea. Her money would be put into a trust to help subsidize children's tuition at a local primary school. As we discussed the prospect, she exclaimed out of the blue, "I will have grandchildren!" She was tickled with that revelation. I told her, "After you go to heaven, your trust will take out a certain percentage per year to fund scholarships, but the principal in your trust should stay there forever and you can help benefit those families in need." To help her with her dream, I introduced her to a lawyer who helped her set up a trust in her and her parents' names. Frieda was so excited when she realized she was creating a legacy for herself. Her name would truly live on.

After the trust was established, I introduced her to a local school that she selected to be the beneficiary of her scholarship. Frieda loved the annual trip to the school and reveled in the attention. The school officials would pick her up once a year on her birthday and take her on a special school tour to be introduced to everyone. Frieda became the school's "grandmother" and kids would send her thank-you letters every year. She was the happiest I had ever seen her.

Unfortunately, about four years ago in 2008, Frieda's lifelong struggle with mental illness became worse. She began calling the police to complain about things like intruders in her home; when the police would arrive, there would be no intruders there. One night, Frieda was picked up by the police after she was found wandering the streets near her home, and she was brought to the hospital. Eventually, she was transferred to a well-known psychiatric hospital in the area. A social worker at the hospital contacted me because one of Frieda's neighbor's had my number as Frieda's emergency contact number. As I mentioned earlier, she had no other relatives outside of her brother, whom she hadn't spoken to in years. It was at this point that a very kind acquaintance got in contact with her brother to let him know that Frieda asked to see him. He said he didn't want to see her. When the acquaintance relayed the message, it just broke my heart. Frieda's worst fears were coming true; she really was alone.

Frieda was in the lock-down ward that was reserved for patients with serious mental illness. Frieda would go in and out of a state of confusion and incoherency. Her social worker and I both wanted her to be properly diagnosed and treated, but Frieda had no medical history because she did not believe in doctors. And as much as I wanted to help with her medical issues, in reality, I had no power of attorney; heck, I was her financial advisor!

Finally, she was diagnosed as having Lewy Body Dementia, a condition that is similar to the dementia associated with Parkinson's disease. When I visited her after her diagnosis, she said immediately, "You are the only person that I trust. Please help me; you promised me you would take care of me." She was just crying for help and I had to agree. She asked me to promise that I would make sure that she was buried next to her parents in Flushing, New York, and I gave her my word. It was at this point that the hospital social worker explained Frieda's two options: either move to a retirement community (which she had already adamantly refused) or go back to her home with around-the-clock live-in care. Frieda just cried and said, "Bob, you have to get me to my home; I want to die in my own bed." She said it over and over again. The hospital referred me to an eldercare consultant group that found a home health care team to help Frieda. She signed the papers and, soon after, the social workers brought Frieda home.

Although as a person, I understood her desire to be in her own home, as her financial advisor, I was cringing. Frieda was spending more than $100,000 a year for round-the-clock home care, and I could see her portfolio quickly dwindling. The home care expenses were chipping away at her assets. At this pace of decline, I also was concerned that her scholarship trust would be in jeopardy, which I knew Frieda would not want. After a year and a half of visiting her in her home, Frieda's social worker and I finally convinced her to move into an assisted living facility. She was worried about moving into a retirement home or assisted living facility because she thought it would be "a dump." But, when the social worker and I brought her to the retirement home we recommended, she smiled and said that it was like a first-class hotel in Manhattan! That smile was precious! I also helped her hire a dependable bookkeeper to help pay all her bills, and at long last, Frieda also hired a realtor to sell her house. The conversation with her about selling her house was very emotional for Frieda. But she wasn't hesitant; she knew it was the right thing to do.

As I write this, Frieda is 82 years old and continuing to decline. But, I recently visited her and let her know that I was writing a book and that one chapter was all about her. Again, I got a beaming smile in return that made all the years of hard work worth it. I did the right thing for her. I made a moral commitment to her, one that went beyond the scope of my duties as a wealth manager, but one that I will see through to the end. I'm glad I didn't give up on Frieda. My team is glad they didn't give up on Frieda. And, I believe that Frieda is truly grateful for what we've done for her. She is content, knowing her legacy will live on long after she is gone.

Chapter 4
Persevere *Even When*
It Gets Tough

When things are going well, it is easy to be motivated and optimistic, whether in your professional or personal life. I have learned that the true test of a person's mettle comes when he or she is faced with adversity. Time and again I have watched as successful people manage to rise above the obstacles and stay the course. The big producers I've known over the years, the advisors who have led the pack, they all share this ability. To be successful, to achieve goals, to conquer challenges; perseverance is what separates winners from the rest of the pack. It takes a lot of determination to persevere, and your reaction to problems or challenges will predicate your success, whether it is as a business owner or as a person. That's why **Principle #4** isn't quite as simple as it sounds. This principle is already inside of you; you just have to tap into it.

In the early 1990's, I was still early in my career as a financial professional. I was working for regional brokerage Dominick & Dominick at that time, and one morning as I pulled into the parking lot at work, I noticed a beautiful Rolls Royce parked in one of the few reserved spots. The car immediately piqued my interest. After a few days of admiring the car from across the parking lot, I arrived early one day and pulled into the parking space next to the Rolls. I couldn't help but be curious about the identity of the obviously wealthy owner, especially since I was working long, hard hours trying to build up my high net worth clientele. So, I placed my business card under the wiper blade on the Rolls Royce's windshield and sat back and waited for the call that I was sure would come.

A week passed, then another. I came in early again and put another card under the wiper blade. Nothing! I couldn't believe this obviously successful Rolls Royce owner wasn't calling me. Week after week, I continued to place business cards on that Rolls Royce and received zero response. Finally, after a year of attempts, I decided I'd give it one last try. This time, I decided to take an extra minute to add a personal touch, and on my business card I wrote, "Please give me a call. Bob Collins." To my surprise (and satisfaction), I received a phone call that afternoon from the Rolls Royce owner's assistant, asking how soon I could be at their offices. I thought, "I am in!"

Upon arriving at the office later that afternoon, I met the assistant in the lobby. As she escorted me down the long hall to "Rolls Royce Guy's" office, I couldn't help but notice all of the beautiful modern art that adorned the walls and furniture. We walked into Rolls Royce Guy's office, and my excitement grew as I saw how luxurious it was. I couldn't help but think of the movie, *Wall Street*, which had been released several years prior, and it flashed across my mind, "Wow, I am in the company of a really big wheeler-dealer!" Just like the Michael Douglas character Gordon Gekko in the movie.

After shaking his hand, I took a seat at the large conference table, and Rolls Royce Guy immediately started peppering me with questions. The first question was why I kept leaving my business card on his car. I told him I wanted his business, and to get his business I knew I first needed to get his attention. It was a simple approach but, with persistence, it worked. Rolls Royce Guy and I talked for a long time that afternoon. In the end, he opened a corporate account and, later on, several personal accounts. He turned out to be a great client, and the experience I gained working with him definitely helped me gather more high net worth assets later on. I truly believe that the perseverance and tenacity I showed while trying to gain his business led me to ultimately winning him as a client.

Of course, I tell you this story to illustrate how perseverance can literally pay off for you in the right situation. With that meeting, I realized that I could go head-to-head with other larger and more successful financial advisors and effectively court sophisticated, educated, high net worth clients. And I realized that I had the confidence and instincts to take my practice to greater heights. One of my favorite quotes is courtesy of Henry Wadsworth Longfellow: *"Perseverance is a great element of success. If you knock long enough and loud enough at the gate, you are sure to wake up somebody."* I believe that's what I did with my business card and the Rolls Royce. It took a year, but it rewarded me handsomely.

Further into my career, I learned that not only is perseverance valuable in winning high net worth accounts, but it is also valuable in winning in a court of law. I have encountered many situations where perseverance was needed in my career, but when the Feds come after you, you need a strong dose of perseverance *and* a lot of aspirin! My run-in with the FBI is something that changed my beliefs about the financial services industry forever.

It was early one Friday morning in 2006, and I was going through a large pile of mail in my office. The stack of mail must have been at least eight inches high. I opened one large envelope that was in the pile, read the first sentence of the letter, assumed it was a class action suit that affected one of my clients, and gave it to my associate to fax to our branch manager.

About an hour later, my client whose portfolio was referenced in that letter just happened to call me. We'll call this client Jim. Jim immediately started asking my opinion regarding a stock, and I said to him, "Oh, I thought you were calling me to talk about the document that I received." And he said, "No, what are you talking about?" So I began reading the letter to him, and when I got to the bottom of the page, I noticed that the last line stated something to this effect: *"The person in question in this matter should not know about this document."* I stopped reading aloud to my client and, as I turned the page, I noticed a judge's name. That's when I realized this was not a simple class action lawsuit notification; it was something far more serious, something *very important*!

Immediately, I told Jim that a judge was looking into his background, and I recommended that he hire a lawyer. I told him I couldn't give him any more information and hung up the phone and right away read the lengthy 15-page document. I read the entire document twice, and as I read, my knees began to shake. The government wanted me to provide records of my client's portfolio because he had a substantial amount of investments with us. I called my branch manager to confirm that he received the document my associate had faxed to him earlier, and I told him that I mistakenly told the client about it. My manager told me not to worry; he would get in contact with compliance, and this should not be a big deal. The government simply wanted information on this client. I didn't feel entirely relieved, and within a day, I knew why.

The next morning, I received a phone call from my firm's lawyer who immediately began questioning me about Jim and the document that I had begun reading to him. The firm's lawyer asked if I knew Jim very well on a personal level. I told him that I had many personal conversations with both Jim and his wife, and may have had a dinner meeting once in a while to enjoy both personal and professional updates on our lives. At the end of our conversation, the lawyer said, "Mr. Collins, there's a good chance your freedom could be taken away." I asked, "Could you repeat that?" He repeated his statement, then added, "You broke a federal law." I told him, "Look, I'm just trying to be a good advisor." I didn't know what else to say. The firm's lawyer was very abrasive and made me uncomfortable.

Immediately after that conversation, I called my branch manager and gave him the details. He said he would get back to me. I had a good track record, a big account book, and I felt confident that the firm would do whatever it would take to help me with this situation. Turns out I was wrong. The next day, I was in the car on the way to see a few clients when my manager called my cell phone and asked me to pull over to the side of the road. He basically said that although he did not agree with the firm's stance, the legal department was in control of the situation, and they were intent on distancing themselves from me, versus supporting me. When I asked what my next move was, my manager replied, "Hire a good lawyer."

So, yes, I was freaking out. Who wouldn't be? I called my wife who tried to calm me down by re-assuring me that people don't go to jail just for "accidentally *reading* things to people." Even though I didn't like him, the first person I called was the firm's attorney; he said he couldn't help me out. I practically begged him to give me some names of lawyers, and he finally referred me to someone. When I researched the referral, I realized the lawyer was a fellow University of Scranton alum! That had to be a good sign, right? I immediately set up a meeting.

My meeting was in a high-end office building just blocks from the White House. The fellow Scranton grad lawyer that I met with that day immediately gave me a weird feeling. He did agree that I had pressing legal issues, but he asked for a large retainer right away. He also advised me to immediately terminate Jim and his family as clients. I just couldn't do that to my client. Jim and his family had been with me for more than 20 years. Even though this lawyer was Scranton alumni, I didn't want to work with him. It didn't feel right.

At this point, I admit I did not feel like persevering. I felt as though I had nowhere to turn; no one seemed to understand. Finally, I went to see Chip Collins, my former manager who hired me at Wheat First Butcher Singer early in my career. I sat in his office with tears in my eyes, explained my situation and asked for help. Chip was the first truly helpful person I had spoken with about this predicament, and he referred me to his friend and lawyer, John Keats, a criminal lawyer in Virginia. I dashed over to Keats' office in Fairfax, about 45 minutes from Chip's office. The office was located in a townhouse development next to the Fairfax County Court House, and so different from the ritzy DC office I had visited earlier in the week. As I walked in, I realized this was no boutique law firm; it was a one-man show.

I told my story to John Keats and explained that everyone I'd consulted with thus far, including my firm's legal department, had been telling me there was a good chance I could go to jail. John had this puzzled look on his face and said, "Why would anybody ever tell you that? People don't go to prison for *reading* something to someone." I thought, yeah that's just what my wife said. And then I asked, "What's the upside-downside?" He said, "What do you mean the upside-downside? There is no downside and there is no upside. This is just a bunch of baloney." I said, "You're HIRED!" His retainer was only $3,500, and I wrote him a check on the spot. While we were still in our meeting, he called the assistant prosecutor on this case as well as the lead FBI agent.

It turned out that the FBI had been investigating this as a fraud case. They had raided my client's home and his offices. They searched everything he owned. The scary part was that they assumed I was in cahoots with my client on the supposed fraud. My team was upset; they couldn't believe this was happening. I tried to reassure them, but the truth was that I was upset too! Every night I was a basket case, but thankfully my wife did a great job reassuring me and trying to keep me focused. Although I heard what she was saying, I couldn't stop thinking, why am I in this situation when I did nothing wrong?

Eventually, I learned that I had to meet with three FBI agents and the assistant prosecutor at the United States Federal Justice Center in District of Columbia. A week before the meeting, John Keats met with me to prep. I felt slightly more relaxed because I had confidence in him at this point. He had me run through my story one time and said, "Okay, we're done. I can tell you are telling the truth, and that will come through to the FBI in the meeting." I left our prep meeting feeling hopeful that just maybe this would all be behind me soon.

A week later, I was at the Federal Judicial Center in DC about to meet with the FBI agents and the assistant federal prosecutor. John Keats and I went through security, rode up the elevators, and walked down what felt like the longest hallways. I saw FBI agents everywhere, as we passed office after office of federal prosecutors. It was like walking through a maze of intimidation. After what seemed like forever, we eventually found the tiny conference meeting room, which accommodated about six people. Seated at the table with me was my lawyer, and on my left was the assistant federal prosecutor. Three FBI agents sat in front of me. I was pretty scared. It was a daunting situation. For the first hour, I gave them details of what happened the day I received the envelope with the document. I discussed my relationship with my client and what I said to him by mistake. They kept interrupting and asking questions about my personal relationship with Jim and if I knew where his money was going, how he earned it, etc. At the end of our meeting, the most intimidating of the three FBI agents sitting right in front of me said, "Do you realize you could have hurt one of our agents?" I said, "What are you talking about?" He explained, "Because you disclosed what was going on to this client, the situation could have become a much bigger problem." I said, "Well sir, I received a document in my office which never should have been sent to me."

In the end, it was revealed that the FBI screwed up and sent this document to my office when it should have gone to the legal department of my firm instead. It was a huge error on their part. When they explained this to me, I responded, "I didn't know what it was then, but now I do, and I hope this never happens again." At the end of the two-hour meeting, the assistant federal prosecutor turned to me and said, "Thank you for your honesty, and thank you for coming down here to meet with us. I want to talk to your lawyer. Would you mind going down to the lobby? He'll be down to meet you in just a few minutes."

I walked back through the maze of intimidation and took the longest elevator ride of my life to the lobby. I couldn't help but think that I must still have some major problems if the assistant prosecutor wouldn't discuss anything else in front of me. After a few minutes, John Keats arrived downstairs. As we left the building, he said, "Case closed. No big deal. They believe you. It's over." You cannot imagine how relieved I felt. It was such a huge weight off of my shoulders to have this issue finally resolved.

You may remember from earlier in the chapter that my attorney's entire retainer fee was $3,500, and that I wrote him a check on the spot. I actually wrote the check for $5,000, as a cushion. Call me a worrier, but I didn't want John to run out of retainer money and have to hold things up while he waited for additional funds from me. When the trial was over, I told him to keep the remaining $1,500 just in case something else came up, but it never did. Two years later, John Keats called up and reminded me that he still had the $1,500. I told him to keep it for a job well done. It was the best investment I've ever made.

Now, when the FBI wants to question you, you don't really have a choice! But, it does take perseverance to stick to what you know is right. If something doesn't feel right, it probably isn't. If you don't like the first or second option, look for a third. That's where you must stay persistent and remain true to yourself. Challenges are going to arise in life and in business. It's inevitable. It is your reaction to these challenges that determines your success. Persistence in the face of adversity is what makes a good businessperson. So, when you find yourself up against the next big obstacle in your path to success, remember that all you need in order to win is inside of you. Dig deep, find that perseverance, and stand up for what you know to be true.

Chapter 5
Follow *Compliance*

Chances are if you have been in the financial services industry long enough, you probably have gripes about your compliance department. Maybe the compliance officers don't allow you to send out your marketing pieces, or perhaps they have reprimanded you on your record-keeping or correspondence files. You may feel that your compliance department, or compliance officer, is not on your side and only seems to create problems. You are trying to make money, and they just keep getting in the way! Am I on the right track? Well, take a deep breath and let me tell you **Principle #5**…COMPLIANCE IS YOUR FRIEND.

I know that seems hard to believe and, trust me, there are days when I don't feel like taking my own advice. But, what

I have come to realize and appreciate over the past 29 years is that compliance is there for three very important reasons. They are in place to protect the client, protect the firm, and protect me—and you. In order to be successful, we need the trust of our clients, and to get that we need compliance. Our compliance departments ensure that the rules and regulations of our industry are followed appropriately. Trust me, the more regulated and respected the financial services industry is, the better it is for you and me. That is why my motto, which I constantly repeat to all my staff, is "make compliance your partner".

However, compliance as we know it today is a relatively new entity. When I was new to the investment industry, compliance wasn't even on my radar. Back in those days, as long as the branch manager approved it, brokers could mail out just about anything they wanted. Things began to change a few years into my career while I was still with Dominick & Dominick. As investment firms realized they needed the protection of an effective compliance department and implemented the necessary changes, a distinct shift in power occurred. Several brokers in my office had run-ins with compliance, and I saw the consequences of not following compliance's rules. As the enforcer of industry regulations, compliance held a lot of power, and they could really bog down your efforts. Quite honestly, I used to get aggravated and think, "How dare somebody behind the scenes tell me how to run my practice, or tell me what's right or wrong." I thought I knew best.

Eventually though, I was forced to concede that compliance's job wasn't in place simply to annoy me! As my business grew, and situations occurred, I realized the rules and regulations that compliance enforces are in place to protect me and my client, and to help ensure that everything I did not only complied with the spirit of the law, but also with the letter of the law… and let me tell you that there are an awful lot of letters in the financial services law. I realized that I needed to totally embrace compliance—make them my "partner". I began to understand that a strong partnership with compliance meant survival in the investment business and should be considered a tool to a successful business.

In my independent world, compliance is crucial. When I was researching which firm I wanted to partner with, one of my main priorities was to find one with a strong compliance department that would support me and help ensure I would not have any legal or regulatory problems in the future. Especially after the trouble in recent years with financial characters such as Bernie Madoff and others who put the industry's reputation and validity at risk, compliance's regulations are more important than ever.

Let me share with you a real life example. Recently, one of my high net worth clients requested a one-page summary of his investments that highlighted the money directed towards taxes, as well as information on his cash flow. I prepared the document like the client requested and forwarded it to compliance for approval. Immediately, they shot it down. Why? Because FINRA rules state I am not allowed to give a client a one-page summary. To protect clients, especially in the wake of recent industry scams, clients must consult their own investment statements to piece together what they want to know.

This might seem like compliance is only making things more complicated for the client and creating more work for the advisors. But the truth is that compliance is looking out for everyone's best interests. And once I realized that I could not provide a one-page summary to my client, I simply decided to meet with the client and go over his statements in person. Not only was I able to answer all my client's questions and provide the analysis he wanted, but it was a great opportunity to have some face time with my client. As a younger advisor, a situation such as this would have frustrated me, but as a seasoned professional I know I need to listen to compliance. You can either let them elevate your business, or you can allow them to bog you down. I choose to let them help me.

Many advisors might not agree with me on this. Some fight their compliance department and then get a reputation for not playing by the rules. But, FINRA made the rules, and compliance is simply enforcing them. As an advisor, you've got to follow whatever FINRA says—they've said it for a reason—and if you go outside those boundaries, I can guarantee it will come back to haunt you. I have enough to worry about. I don't need to worry about inadvertently breaking some arcane rule, too. The advisors who want to buck the system may not have encountered any issues that required assistance from compliance yet, but I have. It is these situations that made me appreciate compliance even more.

As another example, in the late 1990's, I took over a fellow advisor's book of clients when she retired. One particular client that I inherited was a very polite, demure male in his 70's. For the sake of privacy, let's call this client Ken. Ken was very conservative in his investment strategy, so we designed a conservative portfolio that he was comfortable with, mainly comprised of tax-advantaged and potential taxable fixed income and cash flow-producing equities. Ken was my client for more than five years, and things seemed fine; there were never any issues or problems with his portfolio, and he never raised any concerns. I visited his apartment a few times to review his portfolio, and our meetings were always enjoyable.

One morning, I heard from a colleague that there had been a shooting at a local company very close to my house. I didn't think too much of it at the time, but later that night as I was watching the news, I saw my client Ken on TV! Apparently, Ken had befriended a woman who was being verbally abused by her husband and who was caught in a very bad marriage. After years of listening to this woman's stories of abuse, Ken drove to her husband's office and shot him to protect the wife and to restore her honor.

Within days of the shooting, I began receiving phone calls from a close friend of Ken's who had obtained Power of Attorney and who started transferring large amounts of money to family and friends in the Far East. Needless to say, I was extremely concerned about the situation. I alerted my branch manager and my compliance department immediately. They said as long as the proper documentation was in place I had no cause for worry. No cause for worry? Ken's large portfolio was being liquidated within a two-week period, and chunks of $10,000 were being wired worldwide! A murder, money on the move, scandal, and intrigue; it might sound like a good movie, but I was afraid it had the makings of a financial advisor's worst nightmare.

Yet, what put my mind at ease was the knowledge that I had documented everything, including what the Power of Attorney was directing me to do. Knowing that I was in line with compliance, and that all of my documentation was in order, gave me peace throughout the sad ordeal. Ken pleaded guilty and was sentenced to life in prison for pre-meditated murder. Not long after he began serving his sentence, he was found dead in his cell of an apparent heart attack. It was a tragic situation for all involved.

Most of the time when compliance comes in handy a murder mystery isn't involved. Compliance is also there for the more mundane occurrences as well! By the end of the 1990's, the Tech Bubble was just beginning, and I had several clients jump on the dot-com stock bubble bandwagon. One of my new clients at the time, let's call him Sam, was one of them. In the beginning of our relationship, Sam and I discussed his objectives and risk tolerance. We determined he was a middle-of-the-road investor in terms of risk, and that he wanted moderate growth and income for most of his portfolio, nothing too aggressive. With that in mind, we opened two accounts, one with an investment objective of moderate growth and income and one with the objective of aggressive growth. Professionally, Sam was a risk taker—he was a real estate developer by trade, one of the riskiest professions out there—but personally, Sam was setting himself up for retirement. He didn't want to squander all he'd worked for, so we decided he would devote only a small portion of his portfolio to high-risk investments. We took that small account and diversified into a small tech stock. Back then, tech was really booming.

When Sam saw how tech stocks were performing at that time, he wanted to invest more in tech. I told him why I believed that was a bad idea and explained the cyclical nature of these stocks. I tried to put my foot down, knowing his ultimate objective was moderate growth and income, not high risk. But Sam got very demanding. I finally told him the only way I would execute the transactions was if the ticket was unsolicited, and that he would have to put the order in writing. Sam agreed to my terms, and after I received the letter I entered the unsolicited order. Before long, he wanted to do the same thing with another aggressive stock. Once again, I told him that I didn't think it was a good idea and reminded him again of his original objectives. Sam wanted to know why I had this attitude regarding these trades. I told him honestly that I only had his best interests at heart, and didn't want to see him gamble with his retirement investments. But he didn't listen to me and sent me another letter requesting me to place the order unsolicited. You know what's coming next, don't you? It was like watching a train wreck—you can't stop it.

Of course, about nine months later, both of the aggressive stocks caved. And what did Sam do? *He sued me!* His son, an analyst in the telecommunications industry, actually advised him to sue me through arbitration. When I got the word that I was being sued, several corporate bigwigs advised me to "make it go away" and settle. But I knew I had done nothing wrong, and there was no way I was going to voluntary give Sam even two cents of my money.

It took two years for the case to go to arbitration. I was

lucky because, after a lot of research, I had gotten myself a great lawyer. She was exceptional. My favorite part of the entire arbitration process was when my lawyer presented the two letters that Sam wrote to me requesting the unsolicited trades. She had them photographically enlarged to 6 feet by 4 feet. I will never forget how impressive that was! The three arbitrators could see the entire letter word-for-word during the hearings. I really believe those enormous letters (and my lawyer) are what saved me. Sam sued me for an enormous sum of money, but didn't get a penny. I'll always remember the president of our firm at the time calling me saying, "I just got word that you won. I'm proud of you." It was a great feeling to get that call.

Although arbitration is often an uncertain process, I knew that I had not done anything wrong. Fight for what you know is right and don't give in. And remember there is a reason that compliance requires you to document everything! Money brings out a lot of emotions in people, and when there are emotions involved, it is always a good idea to have that documentation there to reinforce the truth. When you run your business in an ethical and honest manner, you have no reason to fear or dislike compliance. Consider the minor inconveniences presented by compliance and then think of a potential arbitration, like mine. I think we'd all rather deal with the small annoyance of paperwork and documentation over a potentially career-ending lawsuit.

As much as compliance is there to help us, the financial advisor, compliance is actually primarily in place to protect our clients. Given all that has occurred in the financial services industry over the past few years, transparency and full disclosure is imperative. Hopefully, this move toward total disclosure should allow investors to again feel trust and confidence in their financial advisors. Since the events that transpired in 2008, self-regulatory organizations have required all fees to be stated in writing to clients. Brokers' and financial advisors' professional background records, while technically always public, are now being mailed directly to any client who is charged an advisory fee on their account. This transparency within the industry should be considered a positive, from every perspective, because every move toward the restoration of our industry's integrity is a move in the right direction.

Chapter 6
Grow *Your Business*

Thus far, I have passed along some of the principles that will help enable you to run a successful investment advisory business. But, this next chapter focuses on more than just another "principle". Now I want to go over several strategies you can use to elevate your business to the next level. If you are ready to truly grow your financial practice, you need to take note. **Principle #6:** You Need Powerful Strategies for Growing Your Business.

The first step to expanding your practice requires you to take an honest look at yourself and your business model. If you are a business owner, you likely already possess some business savvy. But I have found that it takes a deeper, more introspective look at what personal qualities you do NOT possess in order to fully capitalize on your business potential. Look at your strengths and what you bring to your business and to your clients. Then examine the situations where you fall a little short. For example, early in my career I realized that I was not a good public speaker; I knew I could not count on holding seminars to build my client base, even though this was a proven path to success employed by a lot of my competitors. But, what I WAS good at was talking one-on-one with my clients. I had to acknowledge my shortcomings as a public speaker and instead capitalize on what I did well—face-to-face, honest conversations with my clients. This strength has always served me well.

Building your practice also requires some good old-fashioned work. Sometimes getting in front of a client face-to-face requires me to travel a little; sometimes it may require me to travel a lot. But, a foundation of my practice is the belief that each client deserves face time, regardless of locale. That's why I often find myself making the trip to visit with clients in California, Arizona, New York, Delaware, Florida, or any of the other 43 states in which I am licensed. All of my clients appreciate the effort I make to see them, but one client in particular that I recently visited stands out. Al lives in a retirement community one and a half hours north of Tampa. On the day I was to meet with him at his home in Florida, Al's friend asked him if he was interested in playing a round of golf. Al declined, saying, "Actually, I can't golf today, I'm meeting with my financial advisor." When Al's friend inquired where his advisor was located, Al said, "Oh, he lives in Maryland, but he flies down once a year to meet with me in Florida." Al's friend was dumbfounded and exclaimed, "My broker is in Tampa, and he's never made the drive north to see me at my house!" As Al relayed this story to me, I could see how proud he was that his investment advisor took the time and made the effort to visit him. It made me so happy to know that I could make a difference, and that my extra effort was truly appreciated. My only regret was that I hadn't brought my golf clubs with me, because I would have loved to join Al and his buddy on the links.

Once you have evaluated your own strengths and weaknesses, it is time to think about your business. Are you utilizing all of the tools currently available to you through your clearinghouse or firm? Do you even know all the tools that are available? There is a plethora of information and tools out there, but they won't help you if you don't educate yourself on how to best implement them. My go-to tool is Envision®, an investment planning tool available through Wells Fargo Advisors. It is an amazing tool that should be in every investment advisor's toolbox.

Envision® is an investment analysis tool that is favored by my clients and my firm. The Envision® tool continuously looks at a client's net worth, time horizons, and risk tolerance in order to create a plan that can be readily adjusted as circumstances, lifestyle, and/or goals change. I believe it is good for compliance reasons as well because it is yet another source of documentation in the case of a disagreement or misunderstanding with a client.

During the financial meltdown that occurred over the last few years, I was very grateful to have a tool like Envision®. As each day brought about more instability and uncertainty, I was able to address clients' fears about their portfolios in a concrete manner. They didn't need to just listen to my lip service; they had actual written proof. The great thing about this investment tool is that it provides updated information regardless of whatever the market throws someone's way. In that respect, using clients' individual Envision® plan, I illustrated to them how their investments were doing despite the meltdown. During this time, I drastically increased both my in-person and over-the-phone client conversations, as well as upped my out-of-town client visits. My team increased communication with clients across the board as well. All of this was to help put our clients at ease and keep them from panicking. In reality, after our intensified efforts, many clients became more confident they were going to get through this market meltdown despite their portfolios being down. Envision® helped me cement those client relationships, and despite the turbulent years our industry has been through, most of those clients are still with me today.

Another tool I utilize regularly is the annual cash-flow reports that my team and I send out. Each year, we mail reports to clients illustrating the client's current cash flow and offer suggestions on how to potentially improve it in the following year. Of course, seeing the potential for increased cash flow is enticing for any client, so those reports usually generate a lot of calls. Everyone wants to know how to get the most bang for their buck.

Another way to grow your business is by providing good, old-fashioned quality service. I believe my clients stick with me and my team because, no matter what the market is doing, our customer service is always superior. If you want to see your business flourish, offer service that exceeds all expectations. We cannot control the direction of the stock market or interest rates, but I can control the level of service offered to every single one of my clients. I believe that if I provide that, not only are my clients going to stay with me, they are also going to refer me to their friends and associates. That is why, even as my business has doubled in size (and then doubled again), more than 80% of my new clients come from personal referrals. I consider this to be the highest compliment I could receive.

Another excellent, but often overlooked strategy for growing your business is to form mutually beneficial partnerships. Strategic relationships, such as with an estate planning lawyer or a CPA, typically increase business for both parties and elevate the level and breadth of service provided to the clients. Seek out partnerships with professionals that you'd trust with your own business, and make sure he or she is as committed to high quality service as you are, because his or her work will be seen as a reflection on you. That said, over the years I have picked up dozens of new clients thanks to my relationships with a few attorneys and CPAs, and in return I have been able to generate lots of goodwill with current clients thanks to successful referrals I have made.

Now, here's something that you probably wouldn't expect me to say: sometimes an industry merger can be great for your business. Let me explain why. I decided long ago that the only way to deal with change was to embrace it. Mergers are an inevitable part of the financial services industry. If your firm or clearing firm is purchased or merges with another firm, don't think of it negatively. Instead, think of all the additional tools and resources now at your fingertips. Don't get caught up in the noise that surrounds a merger. I've personally been through more than 10 mergers or name changes during my career. Take control of change and make it work in your favor; that's how you grow your business.

With all the various demands on your time as a financial advisor, leader, and boss, you need to maintain your focus. That's why training yourself to stay focused and alert on the task at hand is an important skill you need to develop and nurture. Over the years, I have trained myself to stay focused. Every morning on my ride to work I tune in to CNBC or Bloomberg on my satellite radio to see what the markets have in store. Then, for a change of pace I'll turn up some Springsteen as I pull into the office parking lot. Just five minutes listening to "The Boss" gets my blood pumping and helps me to walk into my office with my "game face" on. I'm ready to lead my team and serve my clients.

With all the hard work you are doing to grow your business, something important to remember is to also take care of yourself. As I have matured both professionally and personally, I have learned that some things in life are beyond our control. I also have learned that while I cannot control what happens, I can control how I react to situations.

Running your own business and being a successful financial advisor is stressful and time-consuming. It would be easy to let the pressure get to you and affect your quality of life outside of the office. But if you let that happen, you won't have time to decompress and focus on other things that are important in your life. Sometimes it is important to just "let it go". Take time for yourself, and allow yourself to do things you enjoy. I hang out with friends and family. Get active by exercising and just working off the stress. I love golf and working out. I like to do activities which require all my attention! That way, I know I am not going to be thinking about work while I am trying to enjoy myself.

Growing your financial practice involves much more than gaining clients and growing your assets. To grow your business in a positive and lasting manner requires strategic partnerships, introspection, and focus, plus the use of the resources and tools that are available to you. Make the most of what your clearinghouse or firm has to offer. Research what is available and learn to use it. Treat your clients to superior service, and they will become lifelong fans, not to mention lifelong referral providers. Embrace change and use it to your advantage. Learn to let go of things beyond your control and make time for yourself and your family. Learn patience. When you successfully incorporate all of these elements, I guarantee that your business will not only grow, it will also flourish.

Chapter 7
Trust *Your Team*

As my business has grown over the years, I have grown with it; both as a man and as a financial advisor. I have always been very independent and resourceful; I was proud of the fact that I could close the deals all on my own. But as the years went by and with a book of business rapidly expanding, I realized that I could no longer do everything myself. That's when I learned principle number seven. I learned I had to invest in more than stocks and bonds; I had to start investing in people. **Principle #7**: Start Investing in People.

To have a successful investment management business, you must build a team that supports and complements you as a person and as a business owner. Equally important, you need to put the right people in the right jobs. As I started to add members to my team, I selected individuals whose strengths complemented, not competed, with mine. Likewise, I knew I needed people on my team who excelled in areas that I could no longer focus on (or areas I was never terribly good at to begin with), such as the administrative side of my business. My team is now eight members strong and is divided into two primary groups: the portfolio team and the administrative team. Of those eight team members, I have several who have been with me for more than 14 years. I believe they have stayed with me for the duration because they know I value their opinions, trust their judgment and offer them growth potential. My newer employees realize that I give them an opportunity to grow professionally and make a direct impression on the firm in the coming years.

My portfolio team helps me manage our clients' assets. They create Envision® reports for our clients using our investment planning tool that I have already spoken so highly of, and they also develop asset allocation reports and perform portfolio analyses. The members of my portfolio team are highly skilled and experienced in their respective areas, some of which are annuities, municipal and corporate bonds, and equities. My portfolio team assists me with portfolio construction, executing trades, and working with clients on a daily basis. I am in constant contact with my portfolio team members, and we have twice-weekly meetings so that we all can stay apprised of the group's assets as a whole. They are intrinsic to my practice, providing me with valuable insights and feedback. Managing such a large book of business would be impossible alone, but with the great working relationship my portfolio team has, we are able to manage the business together seamlessly.

Early in my career, I would not have liked having a team of advisors working with me. I felt that I needed control over all client contact in order to maintain the level of service and advice that I wanted to give. However, in time, I learned how important it is to have a team of trustworthy people on my side. I am able to continually expand my business because I do not need to personally handle every trade and every report myself; I have a team of competent and skilled professionals working beside me. They interact with the clients just as much as I do, and our clients know that they will get excellent service regardless of which portfolio member they work with. Of course, as managing partner, I guide the overall direction of the portfolios, but because I invested in the right people, I am able to step back and allow them to assist me in growing my business.

My administrative team is also imperative in helping me grow my business. In order to manage my group's assets successfully, I needed to delegate more and more, especially on the administrative side. My administrative team is just as important, if not more important, than my portfolio team. They may not be physically entering trades, but they are taking care of something even more valuable. They are the individuals my clients speak to on a constant, and sometimes daily, basis. They are my front line.

Excellent client service is something I am proud to offer our clients. Everyone enjoys high-level customer service, and often we are willing to pay for it. When you are buying a new pair of shoes, good customer service is appreciated. When you give someone your life savings to manage, you should expect the highest service level possible. And the highest level of service begins with answering each phone call with a smile – be upbeat and positive in every client interaction. Clients appreciate that. That's what my administrative team strives for – to deliver the highest level of customer service possible.

Many of our clients come to us because they received poor service from other financial advisors. They hear about my team's high level of service and want to experience it themselves. They deserve it, and our team makes sure they receive it. On the rare occasion that a client has an unpleasant experience with one of our administrative team members, I will personally call the client to inquire what happened and ask what we can do to make it right.

On the other hand, if a client becomes excessively rude or aggressive, it is not acceptable either. My team knows that I trust them and their opinions. If they tell me there is a problem that has escalated with a client, resulting in the client yelling or insulting one of my team members, I will get involved there as well. There have been several clients I have had to speak to about their behavior toward my team members. Usually, by the time I call, they are contrite and apologize for their behavior. There are times, though, when we've had to politely refuse a client's business due to inappropriate behavior toward my team. Each of my team members knows that I trust them and ultimately "have their backs" in such a situation. Fortunately, such instances are rare.

Managing both client expectations and individuals expectations is very similar. It isn't difficult to manage people if you let them have a say in how they want to be managed and mentored. Individuals are just that – individuals. You can't assume they will act like you, respond like you, and want to be managed as you would. You have to mentor these individuals, and you have to be patient with them even if you get frustrated. Make it a priority to meet with your staff on a one-to-one basis regularly. Express your feelings and your thoughts in a calm and respectful manner, not an arrogant way. Keep in mind that the individuals on your team each bring their own personal history and baggage to the table. And remember, for the past ten years or so, working within the financial services industry has been very difficult – for advisors *and* for their staff. I always stress to my team that we're in this together and that we support each other. I am very supportive of my team and want them to succeed and grow within my group.

Even when you are the manager, sometimes your team needs to teach *you* something. Recently, during a closed-door meeting, one of my long-time associates said to me, "Bob, you need to be tougher on the team, and that includes me." This person was right. I was allowing personality conflicts to disrupt the team, and I didn't fully realize it. I finally ended the conflicts by being direct with each associate and letting him or her know what I expected. If the individual is not willing to compromise or change their behavior, the only option left is to let them go. After I decided to end my employment with Wells Fargo Advisors and go independent several years ago, there was one individual on the team who was constantly making errors, and I was beginning to lose trust in that individual. Losing trust in my employee is something I can't have. I explained to this person that after we went independent things had to improve, or we'd have to make some changes. Fortunately, this individual realized that they had to make some changes or risk losing their job. They improved their level of work and regained my trust.

An important thing to consider when you hire someone is to determine where they fit best. I've had to terminate very few associates over the years, and I believe it's due to having the right fit for them in the first place. I like to use a football analogy: my associates are all part of a football team. I'm the quarterback and owner. I have blockers and a defense and offense players. I move the players around where I believe they will excel the most for the team as a whole. Unfortunately, a teammate might not work out in any position; perhaps they are dropping the ball too much. If so, they are "out of the game" and off the team. Okay, this might have lost some non-football fans reading this, but I think you get the picture. Place your people where they will be the most valuable to your team.

Creating a team that works together as a cohesive unit is imperative to a successful business, especially a wealth management business. You have to select team members that have strong skill sets, or those whose potential is obvious. Plus, you need that mix of complementary personalities and strengths. Most importantly, there must be a high level of trust on both sides. You must embrace the importance of every member of your team. And, if you can cultivate a team that works well together and trusts each other, you have the foundation for a business that will grow and thrive.

Chapter 8
Go *Your Own Way*

In addition to being the name of a great Fleetwood Mac song, go your own way can mean many things to many people. For me, and for the purposes of **Principle #8**, going my own way meant breaking off from the wirehouse environment and taking my business independent.

Going the independent route is not any easy decision for any financial advisor, and it certainly wasn't a decision that I made lightly. But there may come a point in your career when you are ready to take that step.

There were numerous reasons that led me to independence, not the least of which was a friend's tragic death in 2007. As I grappled with the reality of a peer's unexpected passing, my mind raced as I thought, "What if that had been me? What if I suddenly died or was afflicted with a major disability? If tragedy struck, what would my family do? What would my team do? Where would my clients go?" I realized I needed to have more control of my business and my career path. The desire for more control grew with each passing day after the death of my friend, and I continued to worry that in a worst-case scenario my wife, my daughter, and my staff would be left to fend for themselves, and my clients would be thrown out to various advisors in the branch or in the region. Most troublesome was the thought of how hard I had worked over the years in this business; to envision my clients being handed over to an advisor they didn't even know or my family not reaping any rewards upon my death was extraordinarily disturbing.

To ease my mind, I went to senior management at my firm and began quizzing them. I said "Here's my practice, I manage one-half billion dollars in assets. What happens to me if I get hit by a bus or have a massive heart attack?" They said, "I hope you have a lot of life insurance." I said, "I do, but my family's life insurance is coming out of my own pocket. I need some security." They told me candidly, "You have a great practice, but you don't have a senior partner or team of partners. This means that all of your clients will be spread out among various advisors in the system, and your team would have to find new jobs." This conversation did NOT ease my mind; it truly opened my eyes to the reality of my situation.

In my role as a senior advisor within a firm, if something happened to me, my family, team, and clients would be at the mercy of the system. I didn't want that. I needed to make changes to help ensure that everyone was taken care of should something happen. My wife and daughter needed security, my team needed loyalty, and my clients needed stability. I knew I had to make a change.

I came to the conclusion that a large wirehouse environment was no longer for me. While the services and support were very instrumental along my career path over the years, I could clearly see that I didn't need their guidance and support anymore. And, quite frankly, I was getting a little bored in the branch atmosphere. I felt I was becoming a number, and I didn't have the control that I wanted. I can get impatient when I need things to move along, especially if it's holding up a client's situation.

I also realized I needed another challenge in my career. Challenges motivate me, and many times challenges create a burning desire to learn and grow—in my life and in my business. I believed I could accomplish these things by becoming an independent advisor; having total control in the independent world would allow me to grow faster and achieve my goals quicker. I researched the independent world, talked to other independent advisors, looked at other firms, and I came to the conclusion that being independent fit my personality—especially at this stage in my life.

As I debated going the independent route, I couldn't help but reflect on the changes I had seen in the industry. Over the years, the number of true wirehouses dwindled down to a select few. Also, the structure had changed. Previously, branch managers were like small business owners within the wirehouse. But in the current environment, a lot of delegation is coming out of headquarters in order to streamline processes and to maintain control. I've worked with great branch managers during my career, and I've also worked with weak ones. But, as time went by and I gained experience, I discovered I didn't need to be managed anymore. I was ready to truly take charge of my career and my team. On April 18, 2008, just 14 months after the passing of my friend, I made the leap and went independent. It was one of the most exciting days of my career.

Exciting as it is, there are caveats to independence. In my opinion, an advisor should not go independent just because he or she thinks they are going to make more money away from the wirehouse environment. If you are considering the independent route, consider the following: will you have the appropriate support network? Do you have the funds to support independence, including the infrastructure and the real estate?

In order to manage the wealth for high net worth individuals or families, you must have a great support system. Using my practice as an example, I have three financial advisors, four full-time administrative associates, one part-time individual, and a nice office in a well-off area in the Washington, DC suburbs. There are significant costs associated with it all. If you want high-end technology, that costs money too. Basically, I am making no more than I did in the wirehouse setting. Managing all of our high net worth families and individuals can't be done "on the cheap".

However, going independent was a lot less difficult than I thought, and one of the reasons was that my firm made it very easy for me to end my employment and go independent. Quite honestly, I gave up substantial monetary (retention) benefits. I also had to pay a certain percentage of first year's gross revenues back to my former firm, so technically I actually *paid* to go independent. But the transition went smoothly, thanks to the firm I went with, and I have no regrets.

Paying to go independent might sound like a real negative to an advisor who is considering this route, but it wasn't a negative for me, and I'll explain why. Despite paying the firm money to leave, the upside is that my practice is now worth much more than what I left on the firm's table. And I believe it's going to be worth a lot more years down the road, which is important to me in the event something happens to me; thanks to the transition, I now feel confident that my family and my team will be taken care of no matter what happens to me. I believe clients will also be in a better situation.

To advisors reading this and considering the move to independence, the actual transition process was very easy for me. This process was time-consuming for my team, but not difficult. I was fortunate because my former company at the time had a division with an independent channel. After researching various independent options, I realized that the independent choice through Well Fargo Advisors Financial Network was actually the best option for me. Their technology, a familiar compliance structure, and a strong company brand cemented my decision to use them as my clearing firm. If an advisor is moving out from under their current corporate umbrella and into another firm's independent channel, things will likely be more difficult from an administrative perspective. It can be difficult, but in my opinion it is definitely doable. No matter what road you choose, it's important to do your due diligence before you make a move and to have the right help. Luckily, I had my team, the independent channel, and an outside consultant helping me with the process along the way. Preparedness and forward-thinking are key components in this transition.

My advice to those financial advisors who are seriously looking to make a move: if you don't have a top-notch support team, don't do it. You must have a good business manager you can trust and another senior person making sure all the accounts are coming over properly. My business manager helped me negotiate my office lease, took responsibility for the bookkeeping and accounting, handled the technology we needed, and set up everything in the office we needed from day one. I delegated all that responsibility and let her take the ball and run with it.   If you think you are going to micromanage a big practice, forget about it. I mean, you could do it, but you have to manage the money and service your clients, too. Delegation is paramount. For me, there was no suffering, no catastrophes, and everything went smoothly. Of course, your experience may differ. My other senior associate oversaw the account and asset transition from the wirehouse to independent. She helped make sure the clients were contacted and their assets were transferred. I am also proud to share with you that 98% of our clients came with us. I was so grateful to my team because everyone reached out and explained to the clients what we were doing and why. The clients wanted to make sure they would still be working with us—they didn't care where we were! We heard, "We are going wherever you are going." The clients didn't seem nervous about the move at all. If you have the right team and desire, I believe you can go for independence!

Of course, making this move to the independent world hasn't been stress-free. With the state of the economy and the financial crises of the last few years, of course clients and employees alike are going to get nervous and frustrated.

Five months into life as an independent practice, Lehman Brothers collapsed on September 15, 2008. The financial world was in complete turmoil, the government was in crisis-mode, and it was pandemonium. I had never seen money market returns under a buck, and historically conservative investments were rapidly decreasing in value. These were all firsts in my long career.

In the middle of these crises, I had to take a reality check—I had to figure out what was really going on. Why were these securities and investments dropping like this? Here I was, 26 years in the business; I went through the 1987 market crash, and the real estate bubble/S&L crisis in the early 1990's. I also went through the Russian crisis, Argentina crisis, the tech bubble, and the 9/11 tragedy. Clients' portfolios had never been as devastated as they were during this time. So I asked myself, "Why is this time so different?" The conclusion I came to was that this time there was a lack of confidence in our federal government, a lack of confidence in Wall Street, and a liquidity crisis. Luckily, the government, the Treasury, and the Federal Reserve stopped that erosion of confidence and liquidity. I held on, and I encouraged clients not to sell. I actually pleaded with them and explained my rationale. Out of the hundreds and hundreds of families and households for whom I manage wealth, I believe it was the right advice. What I focused on were the cash flows, the potential dividends, and interest. At night I would get on the internet reading everything I could about my clients' securities, just to help confirm that they were the right securities for their portfolios. It was a nightmare and it was stressful, especially after all of the hard work of going independent.

This turmoil lasted until April/May of 2009. We all remember that it was a nightmare, and it happened to all financial advisors, regardless of whether they were in the wirehouse or independent world. But, when you're an independent business owner, you have to make all the decisions, and that made it a little tougher. Production was dropping because everybody was scared and hanging on to their cash. And our fees were declining because assets in clients' portfolios were dropping and, as a result, gross revenues decreased approximately 50% in January and February of 2009. I had my usual expenses and overhead, *and* was dealing with the decrease in revenues.

It was at this time that I called an important meeting with my senior associates, and I explained to them that I was about to go against one cardinal investment rule of mine: I was going to dip into principal and into my own back pocket. We had some decisions to make; I had to figure out a way to dramatically decrease expenses because we had no idea how long this would last.

It was crucial that I protected the client service level, but it was tough for me to go against my own advice and touch the principal. My long-standing mantra has always been, "Don't touch the principal", but at the time, I had no other choice. It was "touch the principal" or lay off staff. I was a business owner now, and I had to think like one. I had to protect my practice and keep the level of service up. I certainly did not want my clients to think I was laying off employees—that would have created a bad image in the clients' minds. So, what I decided to do was take it slowly, quarter by quarter, and make up the red by dipping into my principal.

In the end, it was the best decision I could have made. In fact, those experiences as a team only made my group stronger and more committed than ever before. And fortunately, the market bottomed out in March of 2009 and confidence started coming back. As business got back to normal, I sure was glad I kept my team intact and took the risk of using my principal. As a team we now know this; if we can make it through the second worst financial crisis in U.S. history intact, in fact stronger, then we can make it through anything.

If you are an advisor seriously considering a move towards independence, please keep a few more things in mind before you take the leap. First, consider what independent firm you will be joining. The independent firm I chose had many years of experience in transitioning wirehouse advisors to the independent world and did a great job for me, but I know that there are other great firms out there, too. You also want to engage appropriate support. I hired an outside group who worked with my business manager to create a checklist of what needed to be done. Specialists can coach you and your team along the way.

Ultimately, only you can decide if you are willing and ready to make the leap to the world of being an independent advisor. Many advisors are completely comfortable in the wirehouse environment. You don't have to worry about the electric bill, or paying your staff every two weeks, or what happens if the computer network shuts down. But there are those of us who crave the independent world; those of us who are entrepreneurial at heart. For those people, independence is a world you should consider. It provides you with an opportunity to be entirely in charge of the success of your firm. I have never regretted my move to independence, and I am a better manager, advisor, and person because of it.

Chapter 9
Captivate: *Boomers and Beyond*

PRINCIPLE #9 is not a concept or a tool, it is a demographic. And I am going to tell you who they are, why I believe you need them, and why they need you! It is a win-win situation when you bring on the largest demographic group in the history of our country, the group that popularized everything from the hula hoop to the Beatles…The Boomers.

Baby Boomers (those 76 million Americans born roughly between 1946 and 1964) have now moved into the retirement phase of their lives and are looking for experienced and competent advisers to manage their money. A tremendously populated generation, the Boomers are now a wealth of, well, wealth. What are Baby Boomers' needs and characteristics when it comes to investments? What is the best way to approach and court them as potential clients?

For starters, Boomers say what is on their minds. They don't mince words. They appreciate directness and won't tolerate arrogance. This demographic enjoys quality service, especially when it is at a discount. After the losses so many took in 2008-09, they are very focused on never losing big again.

Boomers want to deal with people that will listen to them. They like things simple and straightforward, including their investment advice. And, the truth is, they need you – more than ever.

The fact is, people are living longer these days. That's a great thing. But, most advisers working with the Boomer generation didn't invest their clients' money with the concept of extended and comfortable retirement as a goal. Boomers are likely going to be living in retirement for a long time, and they need their money to last them the duration. Did you know that today's recently retired 65 year-old will need an investment plan to support them in at least 20+ years of retirement? However, the financial crises of recent years have taken their toll on the client's confidence, especially from clients in the Boomer demographic. Between market volatility and the knowledge that retirement is either here or right around the corner, Boomers have a lower tolerance for risk. They have been left feeling vulnerable and are going to look toward conservative and cautious investment advice. Deliver this advice in an easily understandable manner. If a Boomer likes you, he or she will be more apt to do business with you. Boomers need highly skilled and experienced advisors who have been through the market cycles and economic uncertainties over the years; advisors who really understand how to manage clients' money properly. Boomers need cash flow, and they need it to come from dividends and interest—not principal—because as we all know, once you touch principal, it's gone forever, and you can't get it back. Advisors who have expertise in building portfolios around cash flow needs are important, especially when the interest rates are low as they are today in 2012. Boomers need total return (cash flow plus appreciation).

The historic stock market losses of '08 created emotional damage and financial destruction in many portfolios. Still, time needs to be spent on the goals of preserving assets for the next bear market, which eventually will happen, and making sure clients have enough cash flow. I believe the entire investment style must change for Boomers. To add value and to do the best for them, advisors need to articulate how they will help generate cash flow, without throwing everything into bonds, and discuss investing in other income-oriented investments that may include dividend-producing equities, dividend-producing ETFs, alternative investments, closed-end funds, and income-producing securities, etc. Computer-generated pie charts and pretty multi-colored pictures of clients' portfolios don't mean as much to clients as they once did. They want a game plan, and they want to be a part of the game. Boomers are much more computer-savvy than they are given credit for, but they truly appreciate the personal connection of a relatable advisor. And, for most, wealth management is no longer a spectator sport. These clients aren't going to get taken for another ride (after their losses in 2008), and involvement is important to them. There are excellent tools to help clients stay involved. I've already mentioned an investment planning tool called *Envision*, which is one of my preferred tools as an advisor. Clients have embraced this plan that changes as one's position in life changes. It really helped during the 2008-2009 market implosion, and I believe it will continue to help win over prospective Boomer clients in the years to come. Once again, an advisor must have a game plan for the Boomer and be ready and willing to listen to them. If not, they will find another advisory group.

The majority of my clients are managed by myself and my portfolio team; this demographic appreciates this personalized experience. I want my team to be responsible for the performance. The bottom line is that many of today's Boomers need to be counseled as to what is logical in their portfolio and to discuss disciplined risk plans. The typical computer-generated investment allocation model is not going to do it for clients, in my opinion. Graphs won't answer those questions. Boomers need to find advisors who can manage their money in order to pursue a significant amount of cash flow to help them pay their bills, and to help them maintain a comfortable lifestyle in retirement and grow their net worth to keep up with inflation.

So, how do you find a cache of Baby Boomers looking to invest? Well, Baby Boomers are going to search YOU out! Most often, the way Boomers find an advisor they can trust is by talking to their friends or business associates. Having tools such as *Envision*™ to illustrate cash flow generation and portfolio performance in real time will help you land Boomers as clients. Tools like this, and solid investments in cash flow-producing securities, will help these clients to feel comfortable investing with your team.

Especially for this demographic, referrals are our bread and butter. We receive referrals regularly from loyal clients who want their friends and family to benefit from working with a solid team like mine. It can be difficult for those advisors who don't have the longevity, recognition, and track record to garner referrals. But that doesn't mean you should give up. It will just take a little longer; you must be patient. It takes time and trust for clients to begin providing multiple referrals. If you're a younger and less-experienced advisor, my recommendation is to merge your practice with a larger, more seasoned practice. The trend that I see with larger practices with good track records and good reputations is they are getting overwhelmed with demands on their time. And they need help. It seems to be easier for a larger practice like ours to acquire assets from a one-man or two-man team at a wirehouse or independent practices because Boomers these days are demanding a lot more. They want you to help with many aspects of their life.

In order to build a practice and service the Boomers properly, it's important to have strategic relationships with professionals in your community, like CPAs and estate planning attorneys. I have mentioned this business growth strategy before. However, the one thing I'm also discovering is that these relationships can also backfire. Select referrals wisely, because the people with whom you form a strategic relationship with will reflect on you as well.

When you make a referral, (similar to hiring members of your team) you take on an association with that partner which affects their relationship with the client. When forming a strategic partnership, form one where there is trust, professionalism, and experience that can develop into a mutually rewarding business relationship.

Several years ago, I had an experience with a Boomer-aged client that proved enlightening for both me and the client. This client was a referral and was a corporate executive of a large company. His business travel often had him traveling overseas.

When I first analyzed the investment holdings in his portfolio, the securities were all over the place, held at many different institutions (discount brokerages), and there didn't seem to be a game plan. He was trying to build wealth, but he was doing it by himself. This strategy worked during the mid-90s before the tech bubble. But we all know what happened between the 2000-2002 bear market. The Boomer couple came to me after this time period. Their investment portfolio was a mess, they had two children entering college, he wanted to be able to walk away from his job when he decided to, and the couple was frustrated with their financial picture.

My team and I put a lot of time, effort, and care into consolidating the couple's investment assets. We explained our investment philosophy, created an *Envision* plan, and had numerous meetings. By 2008 the couple's wealth was building; we had them organized and on track with a game plan. Our relationship was heading in the right direction. I started to notice that the client was under a lot of pressure from his job, and sometimes it would affect our conversations. So, knowing this client was a high-ranking executive, I chalked his attitude up to stress.

The market began to crack in the late spring of 2008. I told my client and his wife to stay the course because I believed in the investment plan that we had in place, and that it would work out in the long run. Then, the financial crisis imploded in the fall of 2008. My client lost it. His emails became rants and were hurtful and unnecessary, not to mention wrong and unfair.

After many months of receiving this type of correspondence, I decided to have a meeting with my financial advisors and team associates to discuss this client relationship. I told my team that I was considering "firing" this client and explained my reasoning. They were supportive and helped me craft the proper language for my email. After it was sent, I breathed a sigh of relief because I believed that I was doing the right thing by ending this relationship.

When the client's wife realized what was happening, she intervened and asked to be retained as a client. One of my associates stepped up and said that he would take over the relationship, and that we should give the couple another chance. Plus, we could retain the business. I reluctantly agreed.

Over time, things began to change, happily for the better. The relationship is now the best it has ever been.

What is so rewarding about working with this demographic is that Boomers often bring in the next generation of my clients for me. If a Boomer is pleased with the service you provide, they will make sure their children and grandchildren know about you. Heirs to long-time clients will often stay with my team based solely on the positive experiences they have heard about for many years from their parents or relatives. Knowing I am making a positive impact on a generation of investors is a great feeling, and the Boomers benefit receiving professional advice and planning. Like I said, it is a win-win combination!

Chapter 10
Understand *your Portfolio*

PRINCIPLE #10: Understand your own portfolio. Over the years, I have honed a philosophy that I utilize in managing both my clients' assets and my own. I believe it has served us all well through the years, so I thought I'd share some general components with you. Keep in mind that every portfolio and every investor is different, and due to the particular needs of each individual investor, I cannot give specific financial advice. However, no matter what tips or advice you follow, the most important thing of all is to understand your own portfolio. Here are a few tips to help you better understand both your clients' portfolios and your own.

Tip #1 – In my opinion, Warren Buffett is a pretty smart guy. When he talks, it's a good idea to listen.

My investing hero Warren Buffet is famous for his two rules of investing; rules that I have always kept in mind as I manage portfolios for clients, family, and friends:

Buffett's Investing Rule #1: Never lose Money

Buffett's Investing Rule #2: Never forget Rule #1

While losses are not always avoidable, you should be mindful of the fact that losses are absolutely toxic to long-term wealth-building goals. To dramatize this point, consider that if you take a couple of big gambles and experience a 50% loss in a client portfolio one year, it would take a heroic 100% gain the next year just to get the portfolio back to break-even, and that's making the big assumption that the client would even give you a shot managing their portfolio for another year.

In Warren Buffet's 2008 Berkshire Hathaway annual report, he said, "I will not trade even a night's sleep for the chance of extra profits." For me, this means being a careful steward of my clients' money, and being willing to miss out on some speculative potential profits, in exchange for greater confidence that over the long term my clients are better positioned to achieve their financial goals.

I would highly recommend, no matter your investing approach or philosophy, that you become a reader of Buffett's writings. The easiest way to do this is to read the past several years of his Berkshire Hathaway Shareholder Letters, which are available for free at www.berskirehathaway.com.

Another investing role model for me, who is also Buffett's mentor, is Benjamin Graham; he is considered by many to be the father of value investing. No serious investment advisor can consider his or her investing education complete without having read Graham's pioneering book, "The Intelligent Investor". You'll even note that Buffett wrote the introduction to the more recent edition of the book.

Tip #2 – Cash Flow-Producing Securities

My investing strategy stems from the belief that over time, cash flow from investments tends to be more reliable than capital gains. It is not that a dividend can't be cut, or a bond coupon payment can't be skipped, but with careful security selection, it is less likely to happen than a growth stock stubbing its toe and losing a good portion of its value overnight.

Often times, investors think that cash flow oriented securities are only for retired investors who live off their portfolios. In my experience, that simply is not true.

Income can be an important contributor to long-term portfolio appreciation, especially if dividends/coupons are reinvested.

To demonstrate this point, and to help understand the power of compound interest (and something another really smart guy, Albert Einstein, once referred to as the "eighth wonder of the world"), I often use the "rule of 72" to do quick calculations for clients. All you need for this exercise is an estimated annual return, divide that number into 72, and the answer tells you how long it will take to double the size of a portfolio at that consistent rate of return. For example, I find most clients would assume that it would take roughly 14.3 years to double your money at a 7% annual total return (100% gain divided by 7% = 14.3 years), but that is bad math! In point of fact, if you assume a consistent 7% annual total return, with dividends and gains reinvested, the portfolio in question would double in size in approximately 10 years (7% divided by 72 = 9.72 years). The important thing to note in this example is it assumes gains are reinvested (compounded), not withdrawn, so that they can grow over time. I have found clients to be consistently amazed by how powerful the math of compounding can be, once it is fully explained to them.

Now, I know the investment strategy of filling your

portfolio with dividend-rich, income-oriented securities has become less straightforward over the past few years. Bonds are not always the way to go when looking for cash flow-producing securities anymore, but there are many dividend-rich equities still out there for the picking. In my experience, I aim for above average yields (at least 50% to 100% better than mid-term Treasuries), but am cautious of high-yielders (securities yielding more than triple mid-term Treasuries), which can sometimes be a warning sign of a company in trouble, and a dividend at risk of being cut.

By investing in securities that are historical cash producers, I can reinvest the potential dividends or interest for clients, allowing them to compound consistently over time, or, if needed by retired clients, they may be able to live off their potential portfolio income, leaving their principal alone.

Tip #3 – Invest in What You Know

Another all-time great investor, Peter Lynch, was a master of "investing in what you know."

Now keep in mind, "what you know" will vary from advisor to advisor. As I mentioned in my previous tip,

I tend to focus my attention and a lot of my personal research on income oriented securities. That research helped me to develop a great personal research network of local banks and real estate firms (both of which tend to issue higher yielding securities). I frequently have dinner with these guys or join them for a round of golf. From them I can get a sense of which sectors are doing well and which aren't, and as a result, which securities may offer the best, and most reliable, returns over time.

I would highly encourage you to read Lynch's famous book, "One Up on Wall Street" and then set out to develop your own unique area of investing expertise.

Tip #4 – Diversify That Portfolio

Now, I may focus on smaller income producing securities, and as a result those securities may find their way into my client's portfolios more often than they may for another advisor. That said, I also always keep in mind the absolute critical importance of diversification. No matter how good you think you are, some bets will go bad for you, and diversification is one way to help ensure that a bad piece of economic news, unexpected corporate scandal, or surprising sector headwind won't take an unbearably large bite out of your clients' portfolios.

I realize that diversifying your assets is not a new investment idea at all, but it is one I often see clients and beginning financial advisors forget. You see, with 20/20 hindsight, diversification almost always looks like it was a losing strategy. When looking back on the year that just ended, clients always want to know, "Bob, why didn't you have more of my money in that red hot sector last year?" The only thing that changes is what particular sector was red hot! Now of course, if I knew in advance what sector was going to be red hot, I would have been more than happy to plow 100% of their money into it, but the fact of the matter is, my crystal ball is no better than anyone else's!

And don't forget that diversification doesn't just mean diversifying by small cap versus large cap stocks, or stocks versus bonds, or even growth versus value investing. These days it also means U.S. securities versus foreign securities. Make sure you consider a wide variety of options in emerging markets, or Latin America, or even Europe. In my clients' portfolios, some of the types of investments they own are blue chips, master limited partnerships, REITs, global equities/funds, corporate bonds, municipal bonds, preferred stocks, exchange-traded funds, etc.; all play a valuable role in seeking to smooth volatility and improve consistency of returns, a strategy that may not be glamorous in the short term, but I can assure you leads to satisfied clients in the long term.

My first four tips were focused on strategies to most effectively manage clients' portfolios; my next six tips will offer suggestions on how to best manage your own assets.

Tip #5 – Don't Take On Too Much Risk

Clients may berate you after the fact for missing out on the next hot market bubble, but trust me, I believe that striving for consistency will serve your practice far better than shooting for the stars.

Tip #6 – Don't Touch the Principal

I've said it already, but I'll say it again. Don't touch the principal. Don't use it to pay your bills or to fund your lifestyle. Rely on your cash flow to do those things, and leave the principal alone.

Tip #7 – Live Within Your Means

I have seen way too many clients, prospects, and even advisors, who live beyond their means. Don't fall into this trap. Stay humble. Splurge only when you have the money to splurge.

Tip #8 – Give Back

It is important to give back to your community. Give of yourself – both your time and your financial resources. It is just another way to put smiles on others' faces.

Tip #9 – Invest in Your People

Invest in the people who work for you. Pay above the market. Make sure your support staff can see how much you appreciate them in a tangible way. The small amount you put out in paychecks over the years will come back to you tenfold in employee loyalty and performance.

Tip #10 –It's Okay to Be Wrong

One of my goals is to be right most of the time, but I am well aware of the fact that I'm going to be wrong some of the times. It really is okay to be wrong sometimes. Just admit when you *are* wrong. Be sincere. Be humble. Clients don't care about a few wrong picks here and there if you are honest and humble about an infrequent error.

Chapter 11
Create a *Legacy*

One of the greatest joys of being a financial advisor is being in a position to truly help people. I have been fortunate enough to do the job that I love for more than 29 years, and I have never tired of it. Being able to work with people and help them achieve their financial goals is a wonderful feeling. I love to see the smiles of satisfied clients when they feel confident in their financial situation. Simple truth: I love this business. But I also am aware that I am not going to be able to work in this capacity forever. One day, I will need to make a decision about the next chapter in my own life. Whatever I decide to do, in the end there is only one thing that I am sure of: I want to leave a legacy. So, **Principle #11** is Create a Legacy.

Leaving a legacy means more to me than simply passing on my firm. It means more than making sure my family is taken care of after I'm gone. To me, a legacy encompasses those things and more. There were many times during my tenure as a financial advisor when I could have given up. I could have worked fewer hours and cared less about my clients. I could have thrown in the towel during my arbitration or during the (in my opinion) unnecessary Federal investigation, or during the financial meltdown of the century. But, I didn't. I didn't give up because I believe in my industry and in my career. I believe in my team, and in my firm, and in my clients. I believe in, and love, my family. And I believe in my ability and skills as a financial advisor and know that it is these skills that allow me to make a difference in people's lives. Despite the difficult days or on those nights when the plummeting market wouldn't let me sleep, I could never have given up.

My commitment to my clients is something that has kept me going through the years, especially during the difficult ones. Even as recently as the Lehman Brothers meltdown, I knew my clients were the priority. If I focus on their needs and help them with their financial goals, in the end my needs are met as well. For example, during the 2008-2009 crisis, municipal bonds, something in which a significant number of our clients had invested, dropped substantially in value—anywhere from 10% to 40%, due to the liquidity crisis. Brokerage firms, municipal dealers, banks, etc., were not making efficient markets. That meant if a client wanted to sell, they typically had to sell at a price below par value. Investors saw the market values on their statements decline significantly and were alarmed. Because of this, my clients would call me and say they wanted to sell all of their municipal bonds. During this time, I had many opportunities to just sell the bonds and accept the commission, but I didn't. I didn't believe it was the right thing to do. I put the clients' interests ahead of mine, and I'm glad I did.

What's the lesson learned? Many of the municipal bond market values returned to where they were before the crisis, and I retained my clients and my principles. Even though past performance cannot predict future results, in my opinion, when you do the right thing, everybody wins.

Everyone has a skill set unique to him or herself. My skills allow me to be a financial advisor and help hundreds of families achieve their financial goals. It is fun, exciting, challenging, and rewarding. Although at this stage of my career many people ask when I will retire, I know that I am nowhere near retirement yet! Truthfully, I will probably never leave the business entirely—I just have too much fun! Fortunately, I have worked hard and built a team that is as focused and vested in my firm as I am. When the time comes to step back, I will feel comfortable doing so knowing that my clients and my team are in good hands.

For now, however, I am perfectly happy right where I am. What better way to spend a career than by being excited to come to work every day? What better feeling than that of helping people? These are the reasons I love my job, and why I am more excited than ever about the financial services industry. People will always need the help of a talented and compassionate financial advisor, and now the largest generation in history needs our help. People need us! It is our duty to help them secure their financial future and achieve their dreams.

So, what is my advice to fellow financial advisors? Well, I've laid out my best principles of success here in this book. Find your passion. Live it. Breathe it. And persevere. Don't give up—you are your only stumbling block. Make a point to know your clients, their needs, and their dreams. Make a difference in people's lives; realize it is about more than simply meeting your own needs. Know when to follow the rules, when to trust your team, and when to strike out on your own.

If you are already hungry for success, if you already have ambition and drive, get hungrier. Work harder. Keep building your business. The top performers in any field are the ones who keep going, who keep practicing. Think of yourself as a professional athlete—without the vertical jump or endorsement deals. You have to push to better yourself. Natural ability will only take you so far. We all need to work on our game in order to improve it. And if you do work harder and faster and with more passion, I believe you will soon see that the sky is the limit for you and your clients.

In the end, that is the key: when you realize you are helping people and making a difference in their lives, it will put a smile on your face. It's a wonderful feeling. My mission has always been to put a smile on as many faces as I could. Through guiding one family to financial security, I am able to help their adult children, which leads to the grandchildren, which then leads to the great-grandchildren. That's a lot of smiles! And ultimately, those smiles are my legacy.

My sincere hope is that you have enjoyed my book, and it has inspired you. Remember: Principle Matters. Do not compromise, surrender, or abandon your principles; they matter to you, your clients, and the world.

About the Author

As leader of the Collins Investment Group, Bob Collins is deeply committed to acting in his clients' best interests and has received numerous awards for his contributions to the brokerage industry.

Bob has spent two decades as a Managing Director within Wells Fargo Advisors. During this time, he was named a member of the Premier Advisor Program for his high-degree of professional achievement (based on factors including production). As a PIM Portfolio Manager, Bob is among the select financial advisors who are entrusted to manage client portfolios with discretionary authority through the Private Investment Management program. He also serves investors with portfolios of $500,000 or more, and he currently manages more than $575 million for his clients.

Bob lives in Darnestown, Maryland with his wife Beth and their daughter Siobhan who attends Gettysburg College. He is a member of Our Lady of the Visitation Parish and a former treasurer and Board Member of a private K through Eight school.